Healing Plants

Healing Plants

*A Medicinal Guide to Native
North American Plants and Herbs*

Ana Nez Heatherley

THE LYONS PRESS

Printed in the United States of America

10 9 8 7 6 5 4 3 2 1

Design by Desktop Miracles

Library of Congress Cataloging-in-Publication Data

Heatherley, Ana Nez.
    Healing plants: a medicinal guide to native North American plants and herbs / Ana Nez Heatherley.
        p.   cm.
    Includes bibliographical references and index.
    ISBN 1-55821-508-5.
    ISBN 1-55821-509-3 (pbk.)
    1. Herbs—Therapeutic use—North America.   2. Medicinal plants—North America.   I. Title.
    RM666.H33H43   1998
    615'.32'097—dc21
                                                                97-28531
                                                                CIP

Dedication

To my family, past and present, who laid the foundation for this book with their care and teachings. My husband, Timothy Donley, my love, my only love, has supported my work through many years. His care, protection, and encouragement made it all possible.

Life has been an adventure with our children, who mean so much. Jonathan, Melissa, Shane, Julianna, and their partners: Connie, Merechia, and Josh, have stood behind me. And, what grandmother could not mention her grandchildren. I have thirteen in all. They are Joshua, Sean, Matthew, Steven, Kirk, Stephanie, Shannon, Sarah, Jeremy, Amanda, Toby, Erin, Alex, and Ethan. I am blessed.

In Memory

This is in memory of the Ani-Tsalagi (Cherokee) People, who underwent hardships as their lands were taken and they themselves were driven in a forced march to a new territory hundreds of miles away. This has been named "The Trail Where They Cried," for families lost their babies, women, and old ones to the greed of man. The tears were not confined to the Ani-Tsalagi, but they were also shed by some of the soldiers who were acting under orders and whites who watched the sad spectacle.

For many years it was safer to deny one's Indian blood, and much of the culture was lost. But that which remains is being renewed, and the youth are once more proud to be Tsalagi.

—WORDWEAVER

And God said, Behold, I have given you every herb bearing seed, which is upon the face of all the earth, and every tree, in the which is the fruit of a tree yielding seed; to you it shall be for meat.

GENESIS 1:29

Contents

Acknowledgments

There are many faithful friends without whom I could never have finished this book. Davey Wells, a daughter of pioneers with a bit of Indian blood, was one of the first to begin pushing me back to my early teachings. Though she's passed on, she still stands in the foreground of my memories and gives encouragement.

Reed Lewis was invaluable as a consultant, along with Cindi Handy. Thanks to Judith Grace, Jane Toliver, and Billie Rinaldi, who helped with typing and paperwork.

For others who helped by finding plants I needed, I give thanks. Kay, Lee, and Nora Cones took me up Red Mountain, the legendary birthplace of the Kiowa, and a place of great beauty, many plants, and coral snakes. Alice Kennedy and Marjorie Davis offered advice and support. René Weaver and I waded through weeds, took photos, and drove miles to find plants—thanks to her listening, I kept going. Barbara and Steve Benson introduced me to a number of costal plants. Bob and Virginia Lampson took me high in the Sandia Mountains to a hidden wonderland, and Dorothy Butler opened her ranch for prowling and photos.

Harriet Janssen (who passed away in May 1996) along with Beth Swanson and Wilma Mockery served me cota tea, then sumac sauce over ice cream. Later they took me to a mesa in the Southwest's Four-Corners area that was covered with Navajo tea.

There were many who kept me going. I have to mention my appreciation of Kathleen (Anora) Teejen, Victoria (Sparrow) Peterson, Yolanda and Gil Nieto, Jerry Lytle, Roaming Bear and Wild Flower, Sam Haggen, Barbara Benson, Mary Moore, Glenda Smith, and Mildred Bankhead

for their continuous support and faith. There are many more
who helped, and some who never knew the help they gave.
For those not mentioned, please forgive me and accept my
gratitude.

The Beginning of Disease and Plant Cures

In far-off days, as the old ones tell us, the animals, birds, fish, and creeping things, along with humans, could all talk together. They lived in peace and harmony. But this was not to last. The number of people grew and more villages filled the land. The people made many weapons—knives, bows, blow-guns, spears, and hooks. These were used to kill animals to get their meat and skins; others were trampled or crushed through carelessness or contempt.

The bears were the first to rise up against this treatment, and a bear council was called. An old white bear chief presided over the council. After each bear had a turn to complain of how men were killing their friends and eating them, it was decided to begin war against people. There was a discussion then as to what weapon to use. It was decided to use bows and arrows.

Because entrails were necessary to make the bowstring, one bear decided to sacrifice himself for the material. When the bow was ready, another bear took up the weapon and shot it, but his claw caught in the string and the shot went off course. He then had his claws cut. This worked, and he hit the target. The bears shouted, but their cheer was cut short when the old white bear chief pointed out that they needed their claws to dig and protect themselves. "It is best we rely on the weapons we have to protect ourselves," he said. They dismissed the council, and the bears remained friends with humans.

The deer then held a council, with Chief Little Deer presiding. They decided to send rheumatism to any hunter who did not ask pardon for having to kill a deer for food and hide. A message was sent to a nearby Indian village to inform the people of the decision. From then on, whenever a hunter killed a deer, Little Deer, who was very fast, would run to the spot where the deer was killed. He would lean over the blood spot and ask the spirit of the deer if pardon had been asked by the hunter. If the answer was yes, Little Deer left; but if the answer was no, he followed the hunter home and struck him with severe arthritis.

Fish and reptiles held a council to discuss their treatment by man. They decided to give him dreams of eating raw or decaying fish. This way they would have no appetite and would soon sicken and die.

Finally the smaller animals came together and decided in their council to attack man's health until he withered and died. The animals thought of new diseases, intending to rid the earth of mankind.

The plants, who were the friends of man, heard and held their own council. Each plant, whether tree, herb, moss, or grass, offered a cure for the diseases that were to be inflicted on man. Even weeds declared to help. The remedies, however, had to be discovered. Doctors who could listen to the spirit of a plant would be told its cure, and the sick person would be healed.

Learning to Heal

"Come on out and let's go down into Macedony and get us a mess of greens!"

The call was clear and loud from the dirt road outside our house. My mother and grandmother grabbed up pans and knives, and we headed through the door.

Missouri, a large, motherly black woman who lived down the road, was waiting and carried her own equipment for digging. It was one of the first "gatherings" I remember, but they were so alike that they all run together. We'd always go down to the "hollar," as my grandmother said, where a small creek ran. This was our favorite place to catch crawdads.

Had we been here for fishing, we'd have brought an old skillet, bacon, meal, and salt. With a piece of string tied to one end of a stick and bacon and a rock tied to the other end, we'd catch enough to eat. We'd twist their tails off, peel and roll them in cornmeal and salt, then toss them into hot grease. When they were done, we'd fry the cornmeal until it was brown. Mama usually was with us, and that was the best lunch ever. But on this day we weren't there to fish. It was early spring and the greens were popping up.

It wasn't just the fact that we were tired of winter food. The fresh greens were to serve as a cleanser as we ate them, a spring tonic to wash away the toxins gathered over the winter. We'd get what we could beside the creek and in the woods, then head for the low land. Here there were creeks and pockets of water around which we could find all types of herbs: poke, dandelions, lamb's-quarters, and wild lettuce, along with onions and garlic. Later there would be plums, berries, and grapes. As fall came, so did pecans, black walnuts, and hickory nuts. Healing was new in each season, an interweaving of masculine and feminine, life, death, birth, covered with love, and always with prayer.

Healing is an art that one can feel, a gift in which touch and other senses play an important part. (Healing and curing are often two different things. There can be healing without a cure.) Most of us remember the healing touch of a mother, father, or someone else close to us. Mother didn't just feed and dose you. She sat beside you, held your hand, rubbed your back, sponged your head. She brought juice or water and touched you again. When she came with bad-tasting medicine or an uncomfortable treatment, a kiss came with it—another touch.

Once I had been sick and was anxious to get out and look at the new growing things. It was almost spring, and I was always excited with the baby plants showing up. But I couldn't go out. Later in the day, Mama brought in a tin can in which she had planted a henbit that was blooming. That tiny purple flower was probably the prettiest I have ever seen in my life. I saw spring coming, and even at eight years old it pleased me that Mama knew me much better than I thought she did. That meant she loved me. It was a part of my healing. Another thing she did was sing. She sang sleepy songs, religious songs, happy songs, sad songs, and songs of the 1920s. Another way of healing.

Now Daddy was different, but his magic worked just as well. He was the one I called for because I knew he could do anything. When I got sick with sand pneumonia—an ailment common in Texas during the years of the dust bowl—I was taken to a doctor. The trouble was, doctors had no antibiotics at the time, and my father was told to take me home, where I would either live or die. There was nothing more to do. Daddy was logical, and having a scientific mind, he began to think.

If the dust couldn't reach my lungs, he reasoned, I might be able to get well. He wet a sheet and hung it so that it completely covered my bed. The sheet was kept wet. I was only three years old, so I remember little of that part. I do remember, though, that a few days later, when I was doing much better, I heard a bird. It had come into my room to sing and fly around. A perfect gift, a healing gift.

My mother, Katherine, had Cherokee blood, and my father, Gordon, was Cherokee and Celtic. Could two races be further apart? Only superficially. My first thought, when I became aware of my mixed blood, was that I should be torn between two loyalties, or fight myself inside. But the more I looked into the cultures, the closer and closer they came together. Everyone has heard of the Little People of the Celts, but how about the Little People of the Native American Indians? And Stonehenge? In Cahokia, Illinois, there is a structure called Woodhenge, constructed by early Cahokian Indians. Both appear to have a similar function—to keep track of the stars in their seasons. Then I reasoned that it was love that mixed my blood and that I should honor both heritages. I am only one person, after all. It makes sense—one God, one Creator—one blood perhaps?

In my grandmother's garden there were healing herbs growing about the house on equal footing with flowers and hedges. Mama always said that my grandmother could take a bouquet from her yard for someone in need of it at any time of the year. My grandmother, Clara Ann Morris, knew instinctively that all parts of a person needed healing when there was sickness. Her father was a Scottish pioneer who married a Cherokee woman, and they settled in Bosque County, Texas. She was knowledgeable in native medicine and provided treatment for neighbors in the absence of the occasional circuit-riding doctor.

Once, when a baby was delivered stillborn, the doctor handed it to Clara Ann and said, "It's dead. Do what you want." She grabbed up the babe, found a pork rind, and cleaned out the baby's mouth and throat. It coughed, gasped, and let out a scream. Other times she laid out the dead and washed them for burial. Birth, life, and death—they remained the same, and still do.

Even my grandfather, Arthur, had his place. Though he has been gone for many years, the thing I remember about him was his holding me to give me comfort. That memory of love has lasted.

In the classroom, changes took place within me. I was faced with science with its facts. Antibiotics came into being, and everyone's faith was in modern medicine. Traditional medicine was being discounted as folklore or old wives' tales. I began burying my traditional knowledge so no one would see it. We'd all been wrong and had to learn the scientific way. In nursing school, I grew further away from my early knowledge. I seemed to have no choice—it was "either, or," not "add this to your past teachings." But as I grew older and thought for myself, I saw the two types of medical practice—traditional and contemporary—working in complementary ways, rather than antagonistically. Approached with knowledge and respect, they can work together and become stronger for it.

May you enjoy this look at healing plants from the past, understand the benefits of the medicines of today, and watch for discoveries of the future. Although modern drugs usually show a faster relief and herbs take time, I feel that often they are gentler on the body. However, use common sense: In an acute situation, such as a severe infection, pain, or excessive bleeding, modern drugs may be lifesaving.

Should you decide to use any of the plants discussed here, do so only under the guidance of an expert. Using herbal remedies is entirely your own responsibility, undertaken at your own risk.

Gathering
and Preparation

Gathering

The first consideration in gathering plants is safety. Make sure you gather only where it is legal to do so. Make sure the plants are safe from pollution. (For instance, I never gather near a highway.) Know for certain the identity of the plant you are gathering.

Think of the earth and its well-being before taking any plant. Gather only from a large colony and then take no more than a third of the plants. If possible, leave flowers for seed and roots to reproduce next year. Never take more than you need, and do as little damage to the plant as possible. Take clippers along. Keep the gathering area clean.

Preparation

There is commercial equipment to be had, but it is more practical to know how plants can be prepared by using items commonly found in the home.

Equipment for Drying

Most herbs can be hung on a line or laid on paper or flat basket trays. Some of the thicker, more fleshy plants or roots may need air to reach more of their surface area. This can be accomplished by making a suspended hammocklike tray with cheesecloth, perhaps over an open box. Turn the plants frequently if they tend to cling together. If the plant is meaty, like fruit, it can be cut into manageable pieces and laid out on cheesecloth. Pieces that may interest flies may need a light covering of cheesecloth.

Utensils

Use porcelain-coated pots (often called graniteware),
stainless steel, or glass. Pottery is safe to use if it is safe for food.
Use stainless steel, plastic, or wooden spoons. Do not use aluminum or copper. Use the same materials for storing prepared
herbs.

Methods of Preparing

Generally, the plant is washed, weighed, and the water
used in its preparation is measured. I use a small diet scale for
this. The dosages given below are general. Consideration
should always be given to the age of an individual and the type
of herb used. Babies, young children, and older people need
much less than the standard dosage. Keep a written record of
all you prepare.

Compress Make a decoction or an infusion and dip a cloth in
the solution. Place the warm, wet cloth onto the affected area
for about twenty minutes.

Decoction Basically, this means to boil the herb. This is frequently done with roots, seeds, and some of the upper plant
parts, such as leaves, stems, and (rarely) flowers. Use one ounce
(by weight) of dried herb or two ounces of fresh herb in one pint
of cool water. Bring to a boil, turn down the heat, and simmer
for fifteen minutes to one hour, according to the plant: Woody
roots and seeds need to be boiled longer than leaves or flowers.

Dosage: One tablespoon to one-half cup three times a day.

Eyedrops Care must be taken to keep all utensils as clean as
possible. Scrub hands thoroughly before starting. Heat one cup
of distilled water with just enough salt added to barely taste to
boiling. Make a basic tea with the herb and strain through a
coffee filter. If an eyedropper is not available, use a spoon that
has been sterilized in boiling water to drop the tea into the
eye. Solutions prepared for eyes should be made fresh each
time they are used.

Dosage: Several times a day.

Infusion This is a method of making teas or washes. To make a **basic tea** use one teaspoon of herb to one cup of very hot water. Remove from heat, cover, and let stand for ten minutes. Strain through cloth, a coffee filter, or a plastic strainer. According to the plant and condition treated, this tea can be drunk or poured over an affected area.

A **strong tea** is made with two teaspoons of herb per cup of hot water. It should be made fresh for each dosage or kept no more than a few hours.

Dosage: One-half to one cup three to four times a day.

Inhalant Steam, or vapor, has been used over the years to heal. Most frequently it is used for respiratory problems. Healing plants are placed in a pot and brought to a boil. To contain the steam in order to inhale the vapor, place a towel over the head of an adult and the pot, or make a tent by placing a blanket over chairs with the pot underneath. The accompanying sweating is also considered part of the healing. Care should be taken to prevent burning either by the steam or touching the container and its contents.

Oil Infusion After picking the fresh herb and allowing it to wilt, pack it into a jar and cover it with hot oil (any kind of cooking oil will do, including olive oil). Put the lid on and let this sit in a warm place for ten days. Strain off the oil carefully, leaving any water that has collected in the bottom of the container. If a stronger oil is wanted, strain the oil, add new herbs to it, and repeat the procedure. The oil is used topically as an ointment or massage.

Plasters A plaster is basically a poultice. Remember Jack and Jill? Brown paper soaked in vinegar was used as a plaster for Jack's head in the second verse.

Poultices There are a number of ways to make a poultice, but all involve the use of some portion of the herb in direct contact with the body. Parts of an herb (leaves, seeds, stems, or other) can be boiled or simply crushed or chopped to make a

9

poultice. There are those who even chew an herb and apply the chewed mass to an injury. In some areas it is customary to chew tobacco and place it directly on an injury. I have crushed leaves and added a bit of water to them before applying as a poultice in an emergency.

Poultices are frequently used on open wounds, swellings, boils, or sores. The herb may be placed directly on the area to be treated or between two thin layers of cloth to keep it in place. The latter is described under wild mustard, in the next chapter, The Plants. If the herb that is used is irritating (such as mustard), put a coating of grease or oil on the skin before applying the poultice. If the skin begins to show redness, discontinue the treatment.

Salve Tie herbs in a loose cloth bag and place it in the top part of a double boiler. Add one-half cup of lard, vegetable shortening, or petroleum jelly. Heat over boiling water and agitate the bag until it is well saturated with oil. Continue to heat for three to four hours. Add about one tablespoon of bee's wax if the salve is not for immediate use. This will prevent the oil from becoming rancid. Pour into container and cool. If the salve is needed quickly the time can be decreased to one hour, but it will not have the same strength as that heated for a longer period.

Tincture Fresh plants can be tinctured by placing one part herb in a jar and adding two parts alcohol such as Everclear or vodka. Leave the solution in the dark for ten to fourteen days, shaking the jar daily. Strain the liquid off and store it in a dark bottle.

For powdered, dried herbs: Measure and mix 210 cc Everclear with 90 cc pure water (rainwater or distilled water are best). Add thirty grams by weight of the dried powdered herb. Set in a cool dark place and agitate daily for fourteen days. Strain as with the fresh plant tincture.

Dosage: Usually twenty to sixty drops three to four times a day.

The Plants

For the plants that follow, common names (those passed on by word of mouth) are used whenever possible. However, the Latin names are also included since more than one plant may share common names. At times, it has been impractical to use common names altogether and the scientific name is used instead.

Algerita

Berberis, Mahonia

In the hill country of Texas, the Native American Indians of the territory enjoyed the fruit from the algerita. Later, German settlers came to the hills and formed the town of Fredericksburg. There were peaceful relations between the Indians and settlers, and because of this the settlers learned the value of the algerita bush.

Also known commonly as agrito and agarita, this plant shares the area with two other less well known bushes that look similar, with similar prickly leaves. Algerita leaves are compound leaves, with five or seven leaflets. In the spring, the bushes are covered with sweet-smelling yellow flowers and later produce small red fruits. Gathering berries by hand is almost impossible. To avoid the painful thorns, a hide or cloth may be placed on the ground beneath the bush and a stick used to beat the branches, which causes the berries to fall.

Barberries, also in the same family include *Berberis aquifolium* and are found along the Pacific Coast. These have purple fruit. *Berberis canadensis* grows from Canada to Virginia, and a mountain

USED TO TREAT
Chronic indigestion
Constipation
Eye infection
Fever
Mouth ulcers
Sore throat

USED AS/FOR
Blood purification
Food
Liver purification
Local anesthetic

GROWING

The algerita and barberry bushes are used frequently in landscaping. Plants may be bought from nurseries specializing in native plants, or they may be grown from cuttings. They make large full hedges that are colorful during the flowering season or when laden with fruit.

barberry, *Berberis Fendleri*, is common to the Rockies. A European variety, *Berberis vulgaris*, was brought to America by early settlers. It has since escaped cultivation and become naturalized in New England. These plants are used much in the same way.

Medicinal Uses and Preparation

Algerita roots should be gathered during the winter. They may be cut into small pieces and dried for later use. Other woody parts are preserved in the same way. The medicinal parts of the plant are the stem, bark, and root. The bright yellow wood can be made into a tincture and used as a liver purifier or to treat jaundice; the small branches can be made into a cold infusion.

Algerita root may be gathered at any time for drying and made into a tincture or decoction. A decoction can be made by using one-half teaspoon of the dried root to one cup of water. This aids in the reduction of fevers. A wash can be made for inflammation of the eyes. The crushed berries make a tea to treat mouth ulcers and sore throats. Algerita is also considered a good tonic and a laxative.

The flowers, applied to wounds, help prevent infection (Michael Moore, *Medicinal Plants of the Mountain West*).

Food

Algerita is plentiful, and the berries are good for jelly, pies, drinks, as an addition to soups or stews, and for wine. Specialty shops in and around Fredericksburg offer jellies and other condiments made from algerita berries.

Current Interest

Algerita roots are now known to be laxative in action, but weaker preparations are effective in treating diarrhea caused by bacteria, as in food poisoning.

The berry is used for sore throats and acts as a mild local anesthetic. Eyewash can be made from the root. Berberine is the main active ingredient in algerita and is found in other healing plants, such as goldenseal.

Caution

There seem to be no problems with the medicinal or food use of these plants.

 13

YELLOW DYE

Use about three parts by weight (of the root) for one part by weight of cotton or wool. Gather branches or root of algerita and chop into small pieces. Place the pieces in a piece of cloth and tie it closed. Soak the bundle several days in water. Soak fabric or yarn for several hours in water, then squeeze out the water. Immerse the wet cotton or wool in the algerita solution and, stirring continually, bring to a boil. Then simmer until the cotton or wool reaches a color just darker than the desired color. Rinse the material until the rinse water is clear. Dry the dyed material out of direct sunlight.

Aloe

Aloe vera

Seeing a man dripping wet, on his knees, rocking and moaning, was not exactly a sight I had expected when I drove to my son's house.

"He splashed gasoline into his eyes," my son informed me as he opened the car door.

The first thought that came to my mind was: Get him to the doctor immediately. But when I made the suggestion, the man refused. He had already flushed his eyes with the garden hose, but he kept moaning about the burning. That's when I remembered an article I had recently read that told of a doctor who treated his own burned eyes by using the inside of the *Aloe vera* leaf.

When I asked the injured man if he had any *Aloe vera*, he pointed in the general direction of my feet. There were a few small plants, and I broke off a stem, opened it, and squeezed the gel into his eye. Within minutes he was feeling better; within an hour he was working on his car again with the pain gone.

Aloe vera is a native of Africa but has been cultivated in Florida, California, Arizona, and Texas. It has

USED TO TREAT

Bites and stings (including jellyfish stings)

Burns

Chronic constipation

Eye problems

Fleas

Frostbite

Infections

Poison oak

Sunburn

Tissue repair

USED AS/FOR

Shampoo

GROWING

This plant is restricted to warmer climates; however, it is easily grown indoors in a pot in any part of the country.

been reported growing in the wild near the Zapata area of Texas.

Medicinal Uses and Preparation

The plant has long, thick, succulent spikes growing from a central point. These have spiny-toothed edges and are filled with a pulpy gel. This gel is one of the basics of herbal medicine. Many people keep a pot of *Aloe vera* in the house as a source of fresh ointment for burns, eye problems, skin problems, poison oak, sunburn, and frostbite. Cut or break a piece off the end of a leaf and squeeze the gel on the wound. Be sure to use a fresh leaf for each application. The unopened leaf is sterile inside. When a piece is broken off, the part of the leaf left on the plant will heal itself. Not only does *Aloe vera* furnish some action against germs, it also aids in skin rejuvenation. It is probably best known for its treatment of burns and wounds.

The gel of *Aloe vera* is sometimes taken by mouth by those who have chronic problems with their bowels.

Other Uses

Many cosmetics contain *Aloe vera*.

Current Interests

One of the modern uses of *Aloe vera* is to relieve the burns produced from radiation and X-ray therapy. The plant has also been found to boost the immune system. There has been evidence that it might be an answer to AIDS and other viral diseases, and *Aloe vera's* effect on tumors is being investigated.

Caution

The pulp is a well-known purgative but can cause cramping of the intestines and is not recommended for use as a general laxative. However, mixing the gel with fennel may reduce this effect (Michael A. Weiner and Janet A. Weiner, *Herbs that Heal*).

LOTION TO REMOVE WRINKLES

Mix one part of glycerine to six parts *Aloe vera* gel (this can be fresh, scraped from the stem, or the gel may be purchased at most drug stores). Mix no more than a five-day supply to keep it fresh. Shake before using and store in the refrigerator. Apply at night, wash your face in the morning, and apply again. Can be used under makeup. Aloe is thought to act as a sunscreen.

Cleopatra is said to have relied upon the cosmetic use of the aloe plant.

Amaranth

Amaranthus

The tall red amaranth plant with its graceful plumes calls up visions of the Aztecs of Mexico. Amaranth was at one time the main food crop for these people. There is evidence that it was cultivated as long as 8,700 years ago in the Tehuacán valley of Mexico.

Most of the amaranth we see is the smaller green variety, which is usually found in fields, ditches, and waste places. There are usually dashes of red downward along the stem, which explains one of amaranth's common names, red root. Another name is pigweed. It is generally considered just that—a weed fit only for pigs, but a closer look negates this idea. It provides food, medicine, and even color for the garden.

Medicinal Uses and Preparation

The plant is used as an astringent, which means it draws or constricts and stanches bleeding. The dried leaves are used to make a tea to cleanse wounds and stop bleeding. When taken by mouth, the tea helps relieve diarrhea and intestinal bleeding and is frequently recommended for flu symptoms. Other uses are: as a gargle for a sore throat, taken by mouth as a tea for excessive menstrual flow, and as a douche to relieve itching. For medicinal use, the leaves may be picked, dried, and stored for later use.

USED TO TREAT
Diarrhea
Flu
Itching
Scurvy
Sore throat
Wounds

USED AS/FOR
Astringent
Food
Menstrual regulation

GROWING

The cultivated plants are colorful and are often used in gardens. Plants are common in most nurseries, as are the seeds. There are many varieties, such as the yellow or red (about six inches), and the tall, deep red, which may reach eight or nine feet.

Food

Wild green amaranth is not a plant that calls attention to itself. It usually stands upright with lance-shaped leaves that have long spikes on top. The bunches are prickly-looking and often appear as long wagging tails. The cultivated variety is much easier to work with because it is bigger. The large plumes can be taken off when they start to turn brown around the edges. They may then be laid out on a cloth or paper, and the seeds can be removed by pounding and winnowing when the head is dry. The seeds can then be added to a favorite bread recipe or cooked as cereal.

The young, tender shoots and leaves of any amaranth are good eaten as greens and are rich enough in vitamin C to prevent scurvy. Amaranth shoots and leaves are also a good source of vitamin A and fiber.

Current Interest

The seeds have more protein than corn and rice, and possibly even wheat. This, along with the fact that the plants grow almost any-where, make amaranth a good crop to help fight a diminished food supply in poverty-stricken areas. The recent search for alternative food crops that survive in poor soil found amaranth to be a definite possibility (Delena Tull, A *Practical Guide to Edible and Useful Plants*).

Caution

Although most greens (such as spinach) contain some oxalic acid, amaranth contains very little and is safe to eat.

INVASION OF THE AZTECS

The defeat of the Aztec people by the Spanish was due not only to military strength but also to the destruction of the crop the Aztecs were totally dependent on—amaranth.

When Hernando Cortés discovered a stockpile of ama-ranth seeds intended as food for the Aztecs, he knew he held a powerful weapon. The grain was destroyed, and fields were decimated. A penalty of death was imposed on any who might plant or reap the crop. The use of amaranth dye for religious ceremonies was no longer available, and the Aztec people were weakened both physically and spiritually.

Apache-plume *Fallugia paradoxa*

The peach-colored plumes tossing about in the wind look like tiny feathers attached to a headdress, thus the name apache-plume. The flowers are white and shaped like wild roses. The plant is, in fact, a member of the rose family. The colorful seeds of the apache-plume, *Fallugia paradoxa*, are the main attraction. During the growing season plumes are mingled with new flowers, explaining the *paradoxa* of the Latin name (Michael Moore, *Medicinal Plants of the Mountain West*).

This plant is found in the mountainous country from Nevada east and south to Texas.

USED TO TREAT
Cough
Fever
Joint aches

USED AS/FOR
Hair growth

Medicinal Uses and Preparation

The apache-plume is not a major provider of herbal medicine, but it might be available when other plants are not. The roots are harvested in the fall. The bark and flowers are made into tea and used for fevers. Coughs are treated with the tea sweetened with honey. New growth in the spring is considered to be good as a spring tonic.

A poultice for aching joints can be made using hot root tea mixed with enough flour to make a paste. This is then spread on a cloth, covered with a second cloth, and

GROWING

Seeds may be cultivated in the geographical area mentioned above.

applied to the affected area until cool. This poultice may be applied several times a day if needed.

Current Interest

It has been reported that the root and bark tea of apache-plume is a good growth stimulant and tonic for the hair.

Caution

No toxicity has been reported.

COUGH AND DECONGESTANT SYRUP

1 tablespoon dried, shaved root of apache-plume
1 tablespoon fresh or 1 teaspoon dried horehound
1 cup cool water
1 cup honey

Pour water over the root shavings and horehound in a saucepan. Bring to a boil, remove from heat, cover, and allow to sit for 20 minutes. Strain, add honey, and bring to a boil. Reduce the heat and simmer for 10 minutes. Take off the heat. Pour into a jar and keep in a cool dark place.

1 to 2 teaspoons is taken for cough or congestion two to three times daily.

Bee Balm   *Monarda*

USED TO TREAT

Acne

Alzheimer's disease

Cough

Flu

Gas

Headache

Heart trouble

Hysteria

Insomnia

Measles

Parasites

Sore throat

Stomachache

USED AS/FOR

Beverage

Diaphoretic

Diuretic

Hair tonic

Inhalant

Insect Repellent

Perfume

Bee balm, genus *Monarda*, is a native American plant. There are a few nonnative *Monarda* species that have long been naturalized in the United States. They are a type of mint with the usual square stem and minty fragrance, and each variety carries its own flavor. Oswego tea, the common name for *Monarda didyma*, a favorite among the Native American Indians, has a single head and is usually red. The spotted bee balm, *Monarda punctata*, is used more frequently as a medicine, as is purple horsemint, *Monarda citriodora*.

Medicinal Uses and Preparation

Oswego tea is considered to be good for stomach problems, gas, hysterics, flu, heart trouble, measles, to cause sweating, and to help with sleep.

Purple horsemint has a strong fragrant odor. It has been used by the Cherokee as a beverage and medicinal tea. This plant contains citronell, a compound used in some perfumes. In the past, the *Monardas* have been used for worms, inhalants, headaches, stomach and intestinal infections, sore throats, and to decrease water in the system. Spotted bee balm is high in thymol and makes a good antiseptic and is also used in cough syrups and chest

GROWING

Any of the *Monardas* are easily grown from seed or plants, which are obtainable in some nurseries.

rubs. It is a diuretic and helps regulate menses. It is also beneficial in the treatment of the flu and fevers.

The leaves and flowers can be used fresh or dried for tea.

Food

The scarlet Oswego tea, *Monarda didyma,* of New England, served as a substitute tea after the Boston Tea Party.

Other Uses

Bee balm can be crushed and rubbed on the skin as an insect repellent. Citronella candles, which have recently seen a resurgence in popularity, are used to drive away mosquitoes. Bee balm has been rubbed on the skin of Indians and settlers to repel insects. Mixed with oil, they can be made into a hair tonic.

Current Interest

There is evidence that bee balm could aid in the treatment and prevention of Alzheimer's disease (James A. Duke, "Weeds, or Wonder Drugs?").

ACNE TREATMENT

2 ounces by weight chopped bee balm
4 ounces alcohol (Everclear)

Wash bee balm, towel it dry, and place it in a jar. Add the alcohol, making sure the herb is fully wet. Keep in a dark place, shaking the jar frequently. After 14 days, strain into a bottle, cap tightly, and store in a dark place.

After washing and drying the skin, apply the solution to pimples.

Berries

Rosaceae family

USED TO TREAT

Diabetes

Diarrhea

Fungus infection

Gonorrhea

Gout

Nerves

Scurvy

Virus

Wounds

USED AS/FOR

Blood sugar regulation

Diuretic

Food

Increasing immune system

Menstrual regulation

Stimulating ovulation

Teeth cleaning

Uterus relaxation

A Cherokee woman and her husband were arguing for the first time in their recent marriage, and she became very angry. She left her home and hurried away toward the east. The husband felt lonely right away and went after her. He called to her, but she only went faster. Soon the man began to despair and called on the Great One.

The Great One told the man to rest and that He would take care of things. He caused some huckleberry bushes to grow in her path, but she pushed them aside. Next He placed some blackberry bushes with large blackberries in front of her, but she ignored the sharpness of the thorns as she raced on.

Then the Great One decided to appeal to her curiosity and put small plants in her path that she'd never seen before. Peeping out from beneath the leaves were red heart-shaped fruit. These were the first strawberries. This stopped her, and she picked and tasted the fruit. As she picked, she turned to the west and remembered her husband and home with longing. She took her strawberries and ran back to her husband. The woman looked at the berries and

GROWING

Some form of wild berries are found throughout the United States. These plants are easily transplanted, and improved varieties can be bought from most nurseries.

wondered how she could keep such fragile fruit. Then she had an idea. She put the berries in a jar and covered them in honey. This is the tale of strawberries, *Fragaria*, as told by the Cherokees. To this day, most Cherokee wives keep preserved strawberries in their kitchens to remind them of the frailty of love, life, and happiness. Adding a lot of honey is a help in any case (Mary Galloway, *Aunt Mary, Tell Me a Story*).

Medicinal Uses and Preparation

Besides the good feelings that come from eating a juicy bowl of strawberries, this berry's medicinal qualities have been relied upon by Native American Indians for hundreds of years. One of the more interesting uses is to crush the berry in the mouth and hold it on the teeth for several minutes to clean off tartar. Because the berries have a high vitamin C content, they are also used for scurvy and gout.

Treatments with strawberry leaf tea have been used for the liver, for bladder and kidney problems, to calm the nerves, for gonorrhea, stomach pain, and irregular menses. The leaves contain tannin and therefore are good for diarrhea, and as a wash for wounds.

Blackberries and raspberries (*Rubus*) have similar actions. The root tea of blackberries and black raspberries is used as a wash for sores and wounds. Red raspberry leaves are traditionally used to make a tea that is given regularly to an expectant mother a week or two before the birth. This is to strengthen and relax the uterus.

Leaves of the blueberry are used to regulate blood sugar, and aid in the treatment of diabetes. They are also used for urinary infections.

The leaves of all berries can be dried for later use.

Food

Berries are good just as they are and also cooked in a variety of jams, jellies, and pies—to name just a few dishes. Strawberry leaf tea is high in vitamin C.

Current Interest

Tests indicate that the use of raspberry leaf tea may increase immunity, kill fungi and viruses, work as a diuretic, relax the uterus, bring about ovulation, and stimulate the body to produce insulin.

As with any plant that contains tannin, large amounts of leaf tea taken over a long period of time could be harmful.

WHO'S IN THE FAMILY?

A berry by any other name just might be—a rose. That's right. Strawberries, blackberries, and raspberries are in the rose family, Rosaceae. Although the prickles on the stem of a strawberry are not long and stiff enough to cause problems, the leaves and flowers are very much the same as those of other roses. The fruit of several old roses, including the sweetbrier, are large and meaty enough to remind one of the strawberry. Raspberries and blackberries are easier to think of as relations to the rose, for all have grasping thorns.

Strange, such a kinship, but unknown cousins pop up frequently among people, too.

Bloodweed, or Giant Ragweed *Ambrosia*

Imagine intentionally planting ragweed—not just a few plants, but fields of it. That's what archaeologists tell us the early Native American Indians in Kentucky did.

The pollen of both the giant ragweed, *Ambrosia trifida* (also known as bloodweed), and common ragweed, *A. artemisiifolia*, may cause as much as 90 percent of the allergies caused by pollen in the United States. This plant is found throughout the United States, the lower half of Canada, and Mexico. Before or after the pollen production period, it is much less of a problem to allergic people.

The common ragweed is usually small but under certain circumstances can grow up to five feet tall. The leaves are lacy. The giant type can grow up to twelve feet tall with broad, deeply toothed rough leaves. The juice is deep red and can be seen in the stalk in older plants; it was used by the Omaha Indians as a dye. The flowers are bunched on the long stem but are not showy.

USED TO TREAT
Allergic reaction
Bites and stings
Diabetes
Diarrhea
Fever
Gonorrhea
Hives
Infections
Menstrual problems
Mouth ulcers
Nausea
Parasites
Pneumonia
Poison oak
Scalp conditions
Stroke

USED AS/FOR
Astringent
Food
Sedative

27

Medicinal Uses and Preparation

Cherokees have used ragweeds for insect bites and hives and have used the squeezed juice of wilted leaves to treat infected toes (Paul B. Hamel and Mary U. Chiltoskey, *Cherokee Plants—Their Uses: A 400-Year-Old History*).

Other Native American Indian tribes used the plant for the treatment of scalp conditions, diabetes, pneumonia, nausea, worms, and as a sedative (James A. Duke, *A Handbook of Northeastern Indian Medicinal Plants*). Ragweeds have also been used to reduce fever and to treat gonorrhea, menstrual problems, and strokes. The plant is very astringent, and frequently a plant with this property is used for diarrhea, mouth ulcers, and to stop bleeding. It is usually prepared as a tea to wash the affected area and at times is taken internally.

Food

Native American Indians used the seeds of the giant ragweed as a grain.

Other Uses

After the pollen is gone, the stalks can be cut, soaked for several days, and the fibers can be removed. The long fibers can then be woven, used as thread, or used to make rope (Delena Tull, *A Practical Guide to Edible and Useful Plants*).

This plant produces a pale green dye from the leaves.

Current Interest

The plants of the giant ragweed are raised and harvested for the preparation of medication to treat ragweed allergy. The crushed plant has been used successfully by many people to treat allergic reactions to poison sumac and poison ivy.

Caution

Because many people are allergic to ragweed pollen, they might also have an allergic reaction to touching the plant. Because of this, extreme caution should be taken around ragweed. It is not recommended that anyone take a preparation of ragweed by mouth because of the danger of an allergic reaction.

HAY FEVER EQUALS GOLDENROD?

Goldenrod is frequently blamed as the cause of hay fever, but the true culprit is usually ragweed. Although some people are allergic to goldenrod, it is ragweed that is the number-one cause of hay fever in the United States.

The misconception possibly lies in the fact that the two plants bloom at the same time and frequently in the same area. It seems the bright yellow flowers that call attention to the goldenrod have taken the rap for the misdeeds of its neighbor ragweed.

Brier

Smilax

Most people consider greenbrier a weed these days. The Native American Indians, however, both in the United States and in Mexico, recognized it as a source of medicine and food. The vine has thorns, tendrils, and black fruit.

USED TO TREAT

Arthritis

Boils

Heat rash

Itching

Wounds

USED AS/FOR

Anti-inflammatory

Beverage

Delivery of afterbirth

Dye

Food

Sexual effectiveness

Strengthening

Medicinal Uses and Preparation

The upper part of the plant is used fresh or dried and may be powdered.

The Cherokees used the vines to scratch themselves and to rub other medicines onto their skin to treat pains (Paul B. Hamel and Mary U. Chiltoskey, *Cherokee Plants—Their Uses: A 400-Year-Old History*). Along the border and in the Southwest, greenbrier is used by bodybuilders for strength. It has also been used to promote male sexual effectiveness by those living in Mexico and the American Southwest (Michael Moore, *Los Remedios*).

The roots are boiled and taken as a tea for arthritic joints, itching, ulcers on the skin, and to aid in the delivery of the afterbirth. The root decoction is also a treatment for cancer. Wilted or boiled leaves have been poulticed on boils and inflammations.

GROWING

Leave brier plants to the wild.

Food

The tips of new vines, young leaves, and stems may be eaten raw or cooked as greens. Add a little butter and salt.

Some species of this plant are necessary for the making of sarsaparilla, an old-time drink.

The dark blue berries are a favorite of country children. The skins are brittle and there is a slight coating of sweet meat, but it is the next layer the kids like. It is a stretchy, membranous material that can be chewed. This is just for fun, because there is no nutrition involved, but there is nothing toxic about it either.

Other Uses

The whole plant can be used for dyeing. It produces a wide range of colors according to the mordant (a substance to make the color of the dye bright and fast) used and the method of dyeing. Blue-gray is obtained when the solution of water and berries is used with alum in a simmer dye. If you simmer the berries without a mordant, a yellow is produced. When the berries are solar-dyed with alum, a forest green is the result.

The roots give a rusty red when used with no mordant. If a tan is preferred, add alum (Delena Tull, A *Practical Guide to Edible and Useful Plants*).

Current Interest

Brier slows down the growth of cancer cells.

Caution

Some people may be susceptible to skin rash after a scratch by the thorns of the greenbrier. A similar-looking poisonous plant is snailseed (*Cocculus carolinus*). Look carefully—snailseed has red berries and no thorns.

BRIER HEAT POWDER

When the weather is hot and a galled area appears on the skin from chafing and sweating, try using dried and powdered brier leaves on the painful spots.

Broomweed

Xanthocephalum,
Gutierrezia

Broomweed, the common name for *Xanthocephalum* (or *Gutierrezia*), is a description of its use by the early people of the West. Several plants would be broken off and used as a broom, or they might be tied around a stick for more convenience.

Broomweed has other names. Snakeweed is one, because the plant has been used extensively for snakebite. Matchweed is an understandable name, because the plant is very flammable and a useful thing to have around for tinder. There are other names, most of which are unsavory, for farmers and ranchers detest the plant. Broomweed grows in large colonies, using up precious water and therefore reducing grassy areas. Ordinarily, cattle and even goats refuse to eat the plant, and many animals that have been forced to eat it in times of scarcity have been poisoned.

USED TO TREAT
Bites and stings

Malaria

Rheumatism

Snakebite

Stomachache

USED AS/FOR
Delivery of afterbirth

Dye

Fire starting

Medicinal Uses and Preparation

The plant has been used for stomachache, snakebite, malaria, and to hasten the delivery of the placenta. The Navajo chewed the plant and then applied it to bug bites

GROWING

Broomweed is breathtaking when it fills a whole field, and that is usually the way it is found in its wild growth area. Two or three plants grown in a garden from seed is possible, but, because the plants are large, not practical.

and stings. Hopi Indians drank the tea for stomach problems (Reader's Digest, *Magic and Medicine of Plants*). Hispanic people on both sides of the border find relief from rheumatism by bathing in water with broomweed tea in it while sipping broomweed tea.

It is best to gather the plant while it is still in bloom. Break it off at the stem. If one plant is too big to handle easily, snap it into manageable pieces. Make this into smaller bundles by holding the flower end together, folding it fan-like, and tying them loosely around the middle with a string or rubber band. If they are tied too tightly, the plant will not be able to dry. Lay it out on a drying rack, paper, or wide basket. Get plenty for baths throughout the winter.

Other Uses

Broomweed is reported to make a dye that is fairly colorfast. The colors that may be achieved, according to the plant and mordant that are used, are yellow, gold, green, and brown.

Current Interest

Broomweed is used mainly for baths to relieve the pain of rheumatism or arthritis, but it is also kept as a dried decoration. The whole plant may be picked while still in bloom, dried as is, and the yellow flowers will remain through the winter. After the flowers are gone, the dry "skeleton" can be picked and painted, piled in corners, or placed in vases, baskets, tubs, or buckets.

Caution

Keep in mind how flammable the dried plants are when using for decorating.

Because livestock have been poisoned by broomweed, consider this before drinking the tea.

BATH FOR SORE JOINTS AND MUSCLES

Use one bundle of dried broomweed. Put it in a pan, cover it with water, and bring it to a boil. Turn off the heat and cover with a lid. Steep about thirty minutes. Strain into bath water for a soothing soak.

Even though arthritis and similar diseases are not curable, many agree that a broomweed bath relieves the pain. Many drink broomweed tea while taking the bath.

Buttonbush *Cephalanthus occidentalis*

The buttonbush is still used among Native people who know the land and live close to it, but it seems to have fallen into disuse among most other people. Although this coarse plant is not much to look at, the buttons are worth a second glance. The leaves are stiff and rough, but the flowers appear to be round balls with antennae covering them. The antennae are the stamens, and each has a dot of pollen. The whole effect is somewhat fanciful.

USED TO TREAT
Fever
Toothache
USED AS/FOR
Astringent
Diuretic
Menstrual
regulation

Medicinal Uses and Preparation

Native American Indians used buttonbush in numerous ways. It was considered an astringent. A tea was made from the leaf and was used to decrease menstrual flow, as a diuretic, and for fevers. The inner bark was chewed for toothache.

The buttonbush belongs to the same family as cinchona—the plant from which quinine is derived—and except that it is smaller, it looks similar. The plant is used in folk medicine for the same purpose as cinchona (Steven Foster and James A. Duke, *Eastern/Central Medicinal Plants*).

GROWING

Buttonbushes can be found along streams and marshes in most parts of the United States except the extreme Northwest. If you wanted to grow them yourself it would be necessary to reproduce the same environment—very wet soil.

Other Uses

In late summer or fall the flowers dry while still clinging to the stem, and the balls remain. They can be used in dried bouquets.

Caution

Buttonbush contains chemicals that have caused poisoning in animals grazing on the leaves (Steven Foster and James A. Duke, *Eastern/Central Medicinal Plants*).

Castor Bean   *Ricinus communis*

The leaves looked like palm trees high above my head, and I crawled among the plants, suddenly transported to a desert island. The undersides of the leaves were red, as were most of the stems. But it was not truly foreign: This was a forest my mother had planted for me, and at six years old it was exciting to leave my own world and go into that jungle. The seeds look like perfect beans to cook—even if they did look like the big, fat ticks we sometimes found on our dog, King—dark brown with tan spots all over them. But I knew the other side of the castor bean plant too: I knew it was poisonous and was careful not to put it into my mouth.

The castor bean plant, or castor-oil-plant, as it is also called, is a native of Africa. It was imported for landscaping in the northern United States, but it has escaped cultivation and now grows wild in our moderate climates.

Medicinal Uses and Preparation

This plant has been used throughout history. The seeds were found in the ancient tombs of Egypt. At the time of

GROWING

Seeds are readily available in stores and the large plants are an exotic addition to most gardens.

Hippocrates, it was considered a laxative. It has been used topically for ringworm and other skin diseases. The oil is still valued as a strong laxative. Sometimes it is used to quickly rid the body of ingested poisons. Earlier this century it was used frequently to induce labor.

Caution

All parts of the castor bean plant are poisonous. Only commercially prepared oil should be used; there is too high a risk of contamination to try and make it yourself at home. The plant itself can cause skin rashes. As to the poison, there is no known antidote. One seed can kill a child (Lesley Bremness, *Herbs*).

CASTOR BEANS IN EARLY AMERICA

Everyone knows the reputation of the taste of castor oil. *The Dispensatory of the United States,* written by George B. Wood, M.D. and Franklin Bache, M.D. in 1836, gives several ways to take the oil: "Give it floating on the surface of mint or cinnamon water; but . . . we have found . . . the least offensive is to mix it with a cup of hot sweetened coffee . . . Some take it in wine or spirituous liquors . . . When the stomach . . . is delicate, the oil may be made into an emulsion with mucilage or the yolk of an egg, loaf sugar, and some aromatic water. To this mixture laudanum may be added in cases of intestinal irritation."

A KILLER PLANT

Ricin is an exceedingly deadly poison derived from the castor bean. "Its claim to fame is that it was the poison used to kill Bulgarian dissident Georgi Markow in London. . . . [it] was injected from the tip of an umbrella as [he] was waiting for a bus" (Alta Vista Web Pages).

Catalpa

Catalpa speciosa

The catalpa tree can be an amazing sight during almost any season. In the spring the leaves are large bright green hearts. Later, the large flowers, somewhat trumpet-shaped, are white to lavender, with bright yellow "bee guides" leading to the nectar. From midsummer to fall the fruit grows in long pods to about eighteen inches. It changes from green to brown and finally dangles from leafless branches as the leaves turn loose for fall.

The catalpa has been commonly called the Indian bean or cigar tree. Some children have even smoked the pods. It is a native tree, and the Creeks' name for it is *Kuthlapa*, "head with wings," possibly referring to the seed, which has wings on each side. This tree bears the Native American Indian name to this day.

USED TO TREAT

Asthma

Bronchitis

Parasites

USED AS/FOR

Antiseptic

Sedative

Medicinal Uses and Preparation

The bark has been made into tea as a treatment for asthma and bronchitis. The leaves have been used on wounds as a poultice (leave on for fifteen minutes), and the pods and seeds are frequently used as an antispasmodic

GROWING

The tree can be grown from seed, but a tree that is already well started will have a better chance at survival. Catalpa is frequently used for landscaping because of its attractiveness.

38

or a sedative. They have even been used as a vermifuge. The bark and pods can be dried.

Other Uses

The long pods can be gathered or picked up in late fall or winter, split, and woven into baskets.

Current Interest

There have been reports that the tree may offer a cardiac medicine.

Caution

Taking large amounts of medicine made from this tree may cause weakness and vomiting.

Catclaw *Acacia*

The yipping and howling of coyotes jerked me to a sitting position inside my tent. I unzipped the flap to look out, fully expecting to see a half dozen of the critters running around the campsite, but there were none. Coyote is a trickster, but maybe he was calling me to something else. A sweet smell wafted through the tent and mixed with the light of a full moon on the sand and trees. An air of mystery prevailed. What was the odor? It wasn't until the next day that I discovered the source.

Across from the tent was a stand of trees much like mesquite but with more delicate leaves, and round fringed flowers covering the branches. The flowers had the look of mimosa, but these flowers were bright yellow and the fragrance was breathtaking. This was in the Big Bend area of Texas on the Rio Grande River. There was a number of people who were glad to tell me that these trees were acacias, sometimes called catclaw because the thorns on their branches resemble a cat's claws. The plant is found in southwestern areas of the United States and in northern Mexico.

Later I was to discover a grove of another type of acacia that has a double seed pod. These are called

GROWING
These trees are available in nurseries of the Southwest.

huisache (*A. Farnesiana*), pronounced "weesatch," and are not frequently found above the Mexican border.

Catclaw is also grown in southern France and as a commercial crop. The flowers are used in perfume.

Medicinal Uses and Preparation

It's obvious that the tree itself has a calming effect on people, but it also does more. The leaves and flowers when made into a tea provide a good medicine for rest and relaxation that has a sedative effect. It also works well for inflammations of the stomach, diarrhea, and a sore throat and coughs.

The pods and stems with the leaves can be dried and powdered and used as an astringent to stop the bleeding of minor cuts and scrapes and as a powder for diaper rash.

Infections such as pinkeye can be treated with a solution from the pod. The flowers are present during the early spring and can be gathered and dried by laying them out on paper or cardboard. Leave plenty of room for air to circulate around them. The green pods, along with the leaves, are also dried.

Food

The flowers and leaves can be made into a pleasant tea.

Current Interest

The gum from the tree is good for irritated or inflamed mucous membranes. Tea for this use can be made from the small, dried roots.

Caution

Because this plant has an anticoagulant in it, it might not be safe to take during pregnancy.

ACACIA TEA

10 acacia blossoms
1 acacia leaf (the leaf is compound, with many leaflets)
2 cups hot water

Place the blossoms and leaf in a container, pour hot water over it, cover, and let it sit. After it cools, add ice and a little honey. Not only is this tea cooling, it is also mildly sedative.

Catnip   *Nepeta Cataria*

USED TO TREAT

Anemia

Boils

Bruises

Colic

Cough

Diarrhea

Fever

Flatulence

Headache

Hives

Indigestion

Insomnia

Parasites

Stomachache

Teething

Toothache

USED AS/FOR

Diaphoretic

Menstrual regulation

Sedative

Let a cat sniff and roll in the leaves of catnip, and you'll see a very happy cat—an intoxicated cat. Fortunately, this does not happen to people, because catnip is very useful to have around. It is a member of the mint family but does not have the nice scent the other mints have. I think it smells rather mousey.

Medicinal Uses and Preparation

The plant may be picked and hung to dry for later use. It can be made into a tincture by using the fresh or dried plant. It can also be made into a syrup. The tea should be steeped—do not boil.

Catnip is well known for treating colds, fevers, headaches, diarrhea, and as a mild tranquilizer. Other uses include as an antispasmodic, to stimulate menses, and for menstrual cramps. It is also good for sleeplessness.

Many Native American Indian tribes used the plant for medicine, such as poultices for bruises, swellings, boils, and for teething babies.

The Cherokees had their own ways of putting catnip to work: It was given to get rid of worms, for stomach problems, as a treatment for colic in babies, and for poultices (Paul B. Hamel and Mary U. Chiltoskey, *Cherokee Plants—Their Uses: A 400-Year-Old History*).

GROWING

Catnip may be grown from seed or established plants. It is easy to grow.

42

The syrup of catnip is not only good for colds and coughs, but also for hives, indigestion, sweating, and flatulence. The leaves can be chewed for toothache.

Food

Catnip contains vitamins A and C. The leaves may be added to salads. Tea can be made from the dried leaves, and because it has a strong flavor, you might want to add a little lemon. It does have a calming effect.

Current Interest

Catnip has been reported to be an effective treatment for anemia, which is caused by a deficiency of iron in the diet. It has also been shown to be a good treatment for gastrointestinal disorders and menstrual problems (Michael A. Weiner and Janet A. Weiner, *Herbs That Heal*).

Caution

Catnip should not be used during pregnancy because it stimulates the uterus.

OF INTEREST TO CATS

Cats thoroughly enjoy a good tumble in catnip, but not so rats. The strong smell that drives cats wild drives rats away. Other creatures, such as fleas and beetles, have the same aversion to catnip. Sprinkle a few leaves on your cat's bed and it should keep the cat happy and get rid of fleas, too. Place leaves inside cabinets to eliminate rats.

Cattail

Typha latifolia

Roaming Bear is a Cherokee Indian with ties to the Eastern Band of Cherokees through his grandfather. He and his wife, Wild Flower, have a place far back from any main road. Roaming Bear has a lot of cattails down in his cow tank, so when I asked to dig some, he was more than obliging. Digging cattails is not as easy as digging potatoes—it is really messy and cold. I was covered to my elbows with mud and soaked to the skin when he went back to his pickup and got a shovel. That was a big help, and soon we had a pile of the white tubers, many with shoots on them. These I would prepare for eating. The dried heads were ready for picking, but I had no use for them at the time.

Medicinal Uses and Preparation

A few tails had started fluffing and scattering, and I remembered that the Native American Indians diapered their babies with the soft down. The down was saved for that purpose and was protection against diaper rash. The down was also used on scalds and burns. Many people still use it for this purpose.

USED TO TREAT
Boils
Burns
Diarrhea
Diaper rash
Kidney stones
USED AS/FOR
Anti-inflammatory
Food

GROWING

These plants grow easily in water (such as a pond or cow tank) from transplanted roots.

In the spring, the male "tails" produce pollen, which is used by the Navajo and other Native tribes for ceremonies. The young tails have been used for diarrhea. The roots were beaten and used as poultices for conditions such as boils, inflammations, and sores. The more mature roots are full of a starch that is released when the roots are pounded. It is probable that water was added to the beaten roots and used as is or cooked before applying to sores. The roots were also used by some tribes for kidney stones.

Food

Cattail was a major food throughout the country for early settlers and Native American Indians. The young sprouts may be boiled and prepared like asparagus. When the tails appear, each stalk holds a female spike topped by the male spike. These can be boiled and eaten with butter, similarly to corn on the cob. When the male flower turns yellow, the pollen can be shaken into a bag and collected. The high-protein pollen can then be mixed with flour and used for pancakes or bread.

The female spike will turn brown in the fall and puffs will fly off it. Attached to these are high-protein seeds that, with a great deal of trouble, may also be used in bread and cakes. Because it is so hard to pick off the fluff to get to the seed, it has been speculated that early Native American Indians may have burned the fluff off, leaving a roasted seed for eating.

The root may be dug during almost any season, and especially from fall to spring. The roots can be peeled and boiled much like potatoes, and flour can be prepared from the starch.

Other Uses

The reeds and leaves are used in the building of some Native American lodges. In industry, they are woven and made into baskets or used in cane-bottomed chairs.

Caution

The pollen is not highly allergenic, but for people who have allergies to many things, eating the pollen could be risky.

CATCAKES

Thick cattail roots
½ cup flour
½ teaspoon baking powder
1 teaspoon oil
⅛ teaspoon salt
2 tablespoons egg (beat up an egg and measure)

Scrub the roots with a brush and peel the outer layer off. Put the peeled roots in water and pull apart the fibers, working them with your fingers. This will release the white starch within. When all the starch seems to be out, remove the fibers. Let the starch liquid sit until the starch settles, then pour off the water. There should be about ½ cup of pasty starch solution. Add the flour to the starch. Adjust the flour—a little more or less to make a thin batter. Add all the other ingredients and stir until the dry ingredients are just wet. Bake quarter-sized pancakes on a hot griddle.

Century Plant

Agave

The tall century plant reaches fifteen feet or more in height, and as it blooms it also begins to die. The early Apaches and other southwestern Indians could spot this source of food and medicine easily because of its visibility. The century plant, so called because of its longevity, does not actually live a hundred years. It may, however, live approximately thirty or forty years before blooming.

The plant pushes its hard spiny leaves from the ground, forming a rosette of thick leaves that are very sharp. These may grow and mature for many years before the center stalk begins to show. At the top, the stalk branches out, and bunches of waxy-looking flowers appear, reminiscent of a candelabra. As the agave continues to mature, big pods of seed are formed where the flowers were. Then the plant dies. The blooming and death happen in one season.

USED TO TREAT
Arthritis
Constipation
Stomachache
Syphilis
USED AS/FOR
Hair growth

Medicinal Uses and Preparation

Native peoples of the Southwest used the plant in many ways. The root can be used just after digging, or dried for later use. The fresh leaves can be made into a tea by boiling one tablespoon of leaves to two cups of water. This is to

GROWING
These plants may be bought at native-plant nurseries or through specialty catalogues.

aid upset stomach, constipation, and arthritis. It has also been used for the treatment of syphilis and liver disease. The tea, applied topically, is said to prevent baldness.

Food

The root can be roasted and eaten after the outside has been cut away.

Other Uses

Agave can be made into soap by pounding it into pulp after removing the outer layer.

Caution

The tea, if used over a long period of time, may prevent some vitamin absorption. Although fresh juice from the leaves is reported to be an antiseptic that is used topically for burns and wounds, the sap is known to have caustic properties. Skin irritation has occurred among those harvesting agave. As with the handling of any plant, individual sensitivity can be activated. Exercise caution in handling this plant.

AGAVE

Just as the agave is unusually large, so is the size of its pollinator. Where daisies are content with the use of bees, agave uses a larger animal to aid in fertilization: It is the bat, which helps assure the continuance of the plant. The bats either hover above the flower or crawl to them to lick the nectar. In the course of eating, they also pollinate the flowers. There is a certain kind of bat that migrates from Mexico annually just to follow the blooming agave (Reader's Digest, *Magic and Medicine of Plants*).

Chaparral
Larrea tridentata

Hediondilla, which means "little stinker" in Spanish, is just one of the names attached to chaparral. Others are creosote bush and greasewood. The chemicals in the bush retard the growth of other plants.

The plant smells strongly of creosote and is usually no more than eight feet tall. The leaves are olive green, and there is a bright yellow flower. This bush grows naturally in the desert and mountain regions of the Southwest.

Medicinal Uses and Preparation

Many consider chaparral to be a treatment for cancer, and there have been many stories of it curing cancer when all else failed. It has also been used to suppress coughs, help premenstrual syndrome, and treat arthritis. Used topically, it kills germs; therefore, it is good for open wounds.

Michael Moore suggests nightly use of chaparral orally as a tincture or in capsules (made from powdered leaves) for cracked feet or hands, dry skin, or split hair or nails, especially if one cannot tolerate fats in the diet (Michael Moore, *Medicinal Plants of the Desert and Canyon West*).

Chaparral can be taken as a tea, but powdering the dried plant and putting it into capsules or making a tincture

USED TO TREAT
Arthritis
Cough
Dry skin
High cholesterol
Premenstrual syndrome
Splitting hair
USED AS/FOR
Antiseptic

GROWING

This plant is very hard to grow, and few things will grow in the vicinity of a chaparral bush.

may be the best way to take it, because some people object to the strong creosote flavor. Two capsules or thirty drops of tincture at bedtime is the usual dose. Tincture may go down much better in a little water or juice.

Current Interest

Research has been done on chaparral to test its usefulness in the treatment of cancer. The results were inconclusive: About half of those tested showed marked improvement, and others deteriorated.

Chaparral can aid in bringing cholesterol into a normal range.

Caution

Chaparral is not considered safe by the U.S. Food and Drug Administration at this time.

THE OLDEST CHAPARRAL IN THE WORLD?

In the Los Angeles area there is a chaparral tree that is twelve thousand years old, according to carbon dating. This tree is approximately twenty-five feet wide and seventy feet high (Michael Moore, *Medicinal Plants of the Desert and Canyon West*).

Chaste Tree *Vitex angus-castus*

"It's a butterfly bush," my mother told me when I questioned her about the small tree in our backyard. True to its name, it was covered with butterflies of all sizes and colors. The flowers are purple, pink, and white, and the leaves, which are palm-shaped, give off a pungent odor, giving rise to another common name, sage tree. The flowers are more gentle in their scent.

Medicinal Uses and Preparation

The chaste tree (*Vitex angus-castus*) contains a substance from which steroids may be derived and used for irregular menses and problems during pregnancy. This substance is found in the seeds. Tea from the seeds is reported to have sedative qualities; it has also been used to get rid of worms.

Both the leaves and fruit of the chaste tree have been used on the skin for infections and ulcers. The flower buds are thought to be useful in curing pneumonia. Roots are held to be beneficial in loosening congestion.

In the Far East, the berries have been used in the treatment of wheezing, coughs, colds, and abscesses. Smoke from the leaves has been used for headaches. The leaf is supposed to help arthritis. A tincture can be made from the berries, and both berries and leaves can be dried for later use.

USED TO TREAT

Abscesses

Arthritis

Colds

Congestion

Cough

Headache

Parasites

Pneumonia

Problem pregnancy

Skin infections

Wheezing

USED AS/FOR

Menstrual regulation

Perfume

Sedative

GROWING

The plant grows easily from seed or may be purchased from nurseries.

Food

The leaves can be used as a spice.

Other Uses

The flowers, which have a sweet scent, are made into perfume.

Current Interests

The berries have been used successfully to relieve premenstrual and menopausal syndromes.

Caution

High doses may give the feeling of ants crawling on the skin. When using the dried seed, start with just a few berries to judge your tolerance. I have found the berries to be too strong in a basic tea.

UNHOLY DESIRES?

In the days when "magic" potions abounded, most people would seek a love charm or an aphrodisiac, but there were those who had no use for these. Their way of life called for something different—a potion that would erase any feelings of romance or impure thoughts.

Monks in ancient times counted on chaste tree tea to keep their thoughts pure and to remove any unholy desires. Just a story? Possibly, but the seed substance which aids women at their moon time just may provide a source for reducing men's sexual desires.

Chickweed   *Stellaria*

Springtime is often thought of as the prime time to gather herbs, followed by summer and fall. But there is a number of plants that are available in the winter. One of these is chickweed. This plant is actually at its peak long before other plants appear. Because it is a small plant, little attention is paid to it, except by gardeners who find it a nuisance as planting time arrives.

Stellaria is also called mouse-ears, winter weed, and starweed (Reader's Digest, *Magic and Medicine of Plants*). The leaves are the shape of mouse ears, and some types are even furry, whereas others have shiny bright green leaves. The plant is low, crawling along the ground or on other plants. Its outstanding feature is a tiny white flower that has five petals. Each petal is split at the top, giving the blossom a starlike appearance.

USED TO TREAT
Constipation
Itching
Scurvy
Snakebite
Sore throat
Splinters
USED AS/FOR
Anti-inflammatory
Diuretic
Expectorant
Eyewash
Food
Vitamins

Medicinal Uses and Preparation

The plant is usually used fresh but can be dried for some uses, such as as a diuretic. Chickweed has been used for inflammation as a poultice, a tea, or simply by being eaten. It has been used for constipation, to soothe sore throats, as an expectorant, and for bladder infections. It is also good to get rid of excess fluid and a decoction is used for this.

GROWING

This should be no problem. Just make a vegetable garden and the plant will probably show up.

Chickweed is frequently made into a salve for skin problems or itching. The plant can be cooked, spread between two cloths, and applied to painful joints. Oil infusions can be made for use in a bath or can be applied to the skin.

Fresh chickweed juice has been used for drawing out splinters and to treat snakebite. It has even been used by some Indian tribes for cancer and as an eyewash.

Food

Chickweed is rich in vitamin C and is a good prevention for and treatment of scurvy. It can be eaten in a salad or cooked as a green. Because it is very mild, it is good to mix it with stronger greens. Toss a few bacon bits in and serve with cornbread for a great meal.

Other Uses

Fill a jar with chickweed and pour oil (any kind of oil will do; I prefer vegetable oil) over this until it covers the plant. Let it sit for ten days, then use the strained oil in bath or as a massage oil.

Current Interest

Using chickweed for painful joints is more effective for the small joints near the surface of the skin, such as in the fingers, hands, toes, and feet.

QUICK CHICKWEED OINTMENT

½ cup dried or 1 cup freshly chopped chickweed
½ cup shortening or lard

Melt the shortening or lard in a double boiler. Add the chickweed. Keep the mixture over low heat for 1 hour, stirring occasionally. Pour into a container, and the ointment is ready to use. If it is made with dry herbs it will keep well. It will not keep as long if it is made with fresh herbs. Store in a cool dark place.

Cinquefoil

Potentilla

This is one of the magical plants. It was thought in ancient times to afford protection against evil, and especially against witches. Hippocrates could mix a pretty wild potion (which included the proverbial three spiders) to help reduce fever (Claire Kowalchik and William H. Hylton, *Reader's Illustrated Encyclopedia of Herbs*).

There are many species of cinquefoil with common names such as five finger and silverweed; at least one type is found in most states. Cinquefoils are in the rose family, and some look strikingly like strawberry plants.

Medicinal Uses and Preparation

Use all parts of the plant, fresh or dry, and prepare a tea to drink or to use on the skin. Cinquefoil is an astringent plant and is good for a sore throat and sore mouth, including thrush. It also makes a good mouthwash. Cinquefoil works as an anti-inflammatory and is used to treat stomach ulcers. It is good for fresh wounds, minor bleeding, and burns. The plant has been used to treat syphilis, measles, and smallpox. Poison oak can be treated topically with the tea, as can hemorrhoids. Cinquefoil stops pain when used

USED TO TREAT

Burns

Diarrhea

Fever

Hemorrhoids

Measles

Poison oak

Smallpox

Sore throat

Stomach ulcer

Syphilis

Thrush

Toothache

Warts

Wounds

USED AS/FOR

Anti-inflammatory

Antiseptic

Astringent

Mouthwash

GROWING

The stem of cinquefoil grows new plants as it creeps along, just as strawberries do. It multiplies itself without much care, even in poor soil. Some types grow in clumps. Check native-plant nurseries to find cinquefoil. There are few places in the United States, Canada, or Mexico where the plant doesn't grow.

topically. It is mainly for this reason that it has been used on mouth ulcers and to treat toothache.

Food

The roots of cinquefoil are frequently eaten by Native American Indians. At one point, when times were hard, they were eaten in Scotland. Whether they are roasted, broiled, or added to soup they are reported to be excellent.

Current Interest

Studies show that cinquefoil is effective in stopping bleeding. It is also very good for diarrhea and dysentery due to its high tannin content.

Caution

Because the tannin content of cinquefoil is high, overuse could cause kidney damage.

CINQUEFOIL TEA FOR TOPICAL USE

1 well-rounded teaspoon of Cinquefoil Root
1-1/2 cups cool water

Place the water and root in a pan and bring to a boil. Simmer, covered, for 20 minutes. Allow to cool. This tea has been used with good results as a topical treatment for mouth ulcers, as a gargle for sore throats, and to get rid of warts.

Cleavers   *Galium aparine*

This little vinelike plant is found throughout much of the world, but since there is nothing really outstanding about its looks, it is not well known. It goes by the common names of bedstraw and goose grass, but its scientific genus name is *Galium*.

To find this plant, it is necessary to get close to the ground and check out those little creeping vines that grow around the garden, push against the fencerow, or line the edge of the creek. It will be the one that has a row of pointed leaves growing in a circle around the stem at regular intervals. The stem is square with prickles along the corners. There may be small white flowers at the whorls (spokes around the stalk). Older plants will have fruit that is a pair of furry balls.

Although cleavers is looked on as a nuisance by some, others plant it as a ground cover to hold in moisture.

Medicinal Uses and Preparation

The Cherokee, as many other cultures, use the tea to treat gallstones, as a laxative, and for urinary tract infections. It

USED TO TREAT
Burns
Constipation
Gallstones
Gastritis
Poison oak
Skin problems
Wounds
USED AS/FOR
Antiseptic
Astringent
Coffee
Diuretic
Dye
Food
Hair rinse

GROWING
Cleavers is a very aggressive plant in the garden and will probably show up whether invited or not. I never invite it and it is always present when spring rolls around.

57

has been used for gastritis and is well known as a mild diuretic. It is good for wounds, helps stop bleeding, and the juice or tea has been used for skin problems. Because there is no evident toxicity from internal use, it can be taken more freely than some other herbs. Some use the juice for healing burns, treating poison oak, and for areas of weeping skin, even as a hair rinse.

Tea may be made of the leaves and stems. These may be dried, but using the fresh plant makes the tea more effective. Freezing the fresh plant will give you a supply during all seasons.

Food

Very young plants or the young growth at the end of stems can be used as a vegetable. It can be cooked, buttered, and given a dash of lemon juice. Or it can be cooked as a potherb in a mix of other greens.

Other Uses

The roots of cleavers, although small, can be used for red dye, but it would be difficult to acquire enough unless you have an abundant source.

Caution

Fresh juice on the skin may possibly cause dermatitis.

CLEAVERS COFFEE

Gather the cleavers fruit as it turns brown. Roast it until it is golden brown, then pound or grind it into a powder. It can then be used as an instant coffee-type drink.

Clover, Crimson *Trifolium*

Where crimson clover is planted as a cover crop or for the enrichment of the soil, it is among the most spectacular of flowers. In east Texas it grows for miles along each side of the highways in an area that is about fifty feet wide. With imagination, it is easy to see a flowing red river on each side of the pavement. The plants ripple with the wind, giving a feeling of water flowing, a relaxing sensation that points to one of the medicinal uses of clover.

USED TO TREAT
Asthma
Bronchitis
Burns
Cough
Leukorrhea
Sores
USED AS/FOR
Antiseptic
Appetite stimulant
Aromatherapy
Digestion
Food
Liver purification
Sedative
Tea

Medicinal Uses and Preparation

Crimson clover is a sedative and antispasmodic—add this to its sweet odor and you have a formula for relaxation and a good rest. Perhaps this is also why it has a reputation for being a charm to keep away evil. Remember the four-leaf clover?

This is also one of the plants that, although it's not scientifically confirmed, is often used as a treatment for cancer. It is also used as a general tonic to aid digestion and improve the appetite. Crimson clover is considered a treatment for the liver. Topically, the tea has been used on burns, sores, and ulcers.

The Cherokees treated coughs and leukorrhea with crimson clover tea. Many claim the tea is good for any

GROWING

Crimson clover can be grown from seed. It is easy to cultivate.

number of lung conditions, including asthma, bronchitis, and coughs. At one time the flowers were made into cigarettes to treat asthma.

Food

Fresh or dried flowers can be made into a sweet-flavored tea. They can also be eaten in salads or cooked. The stem and leaves may be eaten raw but first must be soaked several hours in salt water to make them digestible. Alternatively, they can be boiled for ten to fifteen minutes.

Other Uses

Clover is one of the best-known and most sought after honeys available, and bees are happy to cooperate in making it.

Current Interest

Crimson clover contains a substance that is now being studied for the treatment of AIDS.

Caution

Diseased crimson clover can be dangerous. And some people can develop a skin rash from handling the plant.

CRIMSON CLOVER COUGH SYRUP

1 ounce fresh or ½ ounce dried crimson clover flowers (measure by weight)
1 cup hot water
2 cups sugar

Place all ingredients in a pan and bring to a boil. Reduce the heat and simmer for 10 to 15 minutes. Strain, pour the liquid into a container, and cap immediately. Store in a dark cool place and use 1 teaspoon as needed for a cough.

Clover, Sweet   *Melilotus*

The wind blowing from the creek carried the sweetest aroma, and I had to explore to find the source. A few bright-colored flowers stood scattered about, but the smell was eclipsed by the continuous promise on the breeze. As I neared the creek itself, there were many tall stringy weeds that stood between me and my object. I entered the weed patch and saw there was nothing beyond except water, and suddenly I realized it was the plants among which I stood that were giving off that special scent. On closer inspection, I saw tiny flowers gathered in a long spike arrangement. This was my first experience with white sweet clover, *Melilotus*. Later, I noticed other sweet clover with yellow flowers.

    It was no surprise to me to find that this plant had been used by many cultures, because its very odor would lift the spirits—a natural antidepressant. In Europe it was put into pillows, and in America it hung in cabins to cheer the spirits and repel the musty odor of dirt floors and mildew. It was hung on bedposts or wrapped in cloth to be laid upon the pillow with the hope of happy dreams to follow. A patch of sweet clover growing in the garden in a strategic location can bring those sweet dreams into the house on a night breeze.

USED TO TREAT

Arthritis

Boils

Depression

Flatulence

Headache

USED AS/FOR

Antibiotic

Anti-inflammatory

Antiseptic

Aromatherapy

Blood thinner

Diuretic

Expectorant

Emollient

Sedative

GROWING

Check with nurseries that specialize in wild flowers, or collect seeds in the late summer for planting. Sweet clover grows well in many types of soil.

61

Medicinal Uses and Preparation

The scent of sweet clover becomes stronger as the plant dries, and sweet clover must be dried before use. The plant is picked when its flowers and leaves are thickest. It is frequently used as a flavoring that is very much like vanilla; in Mexico, it is actually used to make vanilla. It can be drunk as a relaxing tea—the leaf tea has the reputation of being a mild sedative and a cure for headaches. Dried seeds, which are rich in protein, have been added to stews and soups. It has been used in making wine and is an ingredient in Polish vodka.

Sweet clover is an expectorant and emollient. It is used as a poultice on inflamed areas because it is antiseptic. Some have used the seed as an antibiotic. Cherokees and settlers used it as a diuretic. A decoction was made of the plant and applied to the sore breasts of new mothers. It has the reputation of settling the stomach and reducing flatulence. Sweet clover ointment has been made for boils, arthritis, and swellings.

Current Interest

There have been some scientific investigations into the possibility that *Melilotus* could be used as an anticoagulant for treating blood clots.

Caution

The plant contains an anticoagulant, which thins the blood and reduces clotting. It is not safe for long-term use and should not be used during pregnancy. Care should be exercised when taking it along with prescription drugs; those taking blood thinners or free bleeders should not use sweet clover. Large doses may cause vomiting. Care must be taken to use only healthy plants, which should be hung individually and dried thoroughly.

CLOVER BUNDLES FOR THE HOUSE

After drying sweet clover plants, break them down to make smaller bundles. These can be very small—three to four inches in length, up to eight to ten inches. They can be tied with something attractive, such as leather or ribbons. Items such as beads, feathers, or seeds might be added. The bundles can be used at home, given as gifts, or hung in the bedroom just for comfort.

Cocklebur *Xanthium strumarium*

In the early days of the Cherokee, stickers of all types, including cocklebur, were considered to have unusual powers because of their ability to hold on to things. It was felt they could improve one's memory, thus producing a stable character. After the birth of a baby, stickers of a small type were beaten and added to water from a moving source, such as a waterfall. This mixture was put in a bowl and given to the child to drink four days in a row. The noise of the water was considered the voice of the river spirit, which would teach the child. The moving water of the river had the ability to seize and hold anything put upon it. Thus, after this ceremony, the child would be able to learn quickly and retain what was learned (James Mooney. *James Mooney's History, Myths, and Sacred Formulas of the Cherokee*).

USED TO TREAT
Arthritis
Cramps
Croup
Diarrhea
Tuberculosis

USED AS/FOR
Analgesic
Antiseptic
Antispasmodic
Astringent
Deodorant
Diuretic
Lamp oil

Medicinal Uses and Preparation

Many Native American Indian tribes use the cocklebur as a medicinal plant. The Cherokee use cocklebur tea for

GROWING

I think it would cause more problems than it is worth. As Michael Moore writes, and I agree, "Avoid cultivation at all costs."

The pods of the cocklebur are the size of a thumb and covered with barbed stickers. If you get one in your hand or foot it can be very painful to get out, like a lot of miniature fish hooks. The burrs also get caught in the hair and clothing. Your garden would soon be covered with cocklebur, and there are plenty to be found in the wild. Although the plant is somewhat attractive, it has no flowers to speak of.

cramps, as a diuretic, and for bladder infections. Other tribes make root tea for croup. The leaf tea is thought to help in tuberculosis, arthritis, and diarrhea. Crushed, boiled pods are analgesic, diuretic, and antispasmodic in effect and have been used for arthritis. Cocklebur is also used to treat wounds and stop bleeding (Michael Moore, *Medicinal Plants of the Mountain West*).

Other Uses

There is little use for cockleburs other than its medicinal uses, though I know that the burrs have been processed to produce oil for lamps, and one Southwest Indian tribe is reputed to have used the plant as an underarm deodorant.

Caution

Cocklebur can be toxic, affecting the liver or possibly causing trouble with the gastrointestinal system.

COCKLEBUR TEA FOR DIARRHEA

4 cocklebur pods
2 cups cold water

Wash the burrs and place them with 2 cups of water in a pan and cover. Place on heat and boil for 4 or 5 minutes. Strain and add enough water to make 2 cups of liquid. Take by sips for diarrhea.

Coneflower
Echinacea

One of the most complete medicinal plants that is native to the United States is *Echinacea*. There are many species, but *E. angustifolia*, *E. purpurea*, and *E. pallida* are the main medicinal plants. They were used extensively by Native American Indians. When the early settlers arrived, the virtues of the coneflower were passed on to the newcomers.

Medicinal Uses and Preparation

The plant juice is said to have the power to prevent burning if the hands are washed in it and then thrust into hot water. A Winnebago is said to have used the juice as a mouthwash before putting hot coals into his mouth (Michael Moore, *Medicinal Plants of the Desert and Canyon West*). Whether that particular burn prevention was effective or not, it is a fact that *Echinacea* works well on burns.

 Echinacea is also used for infections, abscesses, urinary tract infections, skin conditions, sore throats, mouth ulcers, septicemia, tuberculosis, wounds, colds, ear infections, flu, ulcers, and all types of bites and tumors—including cancerous ones.

 Echinacea decreases swelling in damaged joints caused by injury or disease. It can be made into a tea or a tincture using either the flower or the root. (There are those who

USED TO TREAT
Abscesses
Bites
Burns
Colds
Earache
Flu
Herpes
Infection
Mouth ulcers
Septicemia
Skin problems
Sore throat
Tuberculosis
Tumors
Urinary tract infection
Virus
Wounds
USED AS/FOR
Antiseptic
Anti-inflammatory
Increasing immune system

GROWING

The coneflower is found in the south-central and southwestern United States. *Echinacea* is widely used in landscaping and looks very much like a pink daisy, which is another common name for it. It is easily grown from seed or by root division. Usually when I dig a plant, I take all the small plants off the large root and replant them. It takes about three years to get roots that are big enough to work with.

65

use any part of the plant.) Regular-strength tea is effective, or the tincture can be put into juice to make it more palatable. I relied on this to decrease swelling and pain when I broke my ankle. I took sixty drops three to four times a day, and it worked very well.

Current Interest

Scientific studies have shown most of the medicinal uses of *Echinacea* to be effective. The immune system is stimulated by the use of *Echinacea*. It works against tumors and viruses, including herpes and influenza (Michael A. Weiner and Janet A. Weiner, *Herbs That Heal*).

There have been tests using *Echinacea* on children with ear infections that show a high success rate.

Caution

Echinacea should not be taken on a regular basis, rather it should be taken when you are exposed to an infection, or to treat a condition. Constant use may weaken the body's own natural immune response.

Copper Canyon Marigold

Tagetes lucida

My first plant of copper canyon marigold, or sweet marigold, was a small thing. Its leaves were thin and toothed, and I planted it near the sidewalk, where it wouldn't get lost among some of the larger plants. I needn't have worried. It grew and grew until it sprawled nearly halfway across the sidewalk. It reached my chest, and one touch against a leaf brought a powerful minty odor. I had given up on blooms by then, and then, in November, it was suddenly covered with small yellow blossoms. It was a showy plant.

It comes from Mexico, where it is called *yerba anis*, the same name I've heard the anis plant called. It is used by the Tarahumara people of the Copper Canyon region of Mexico. I predict it will be naturalized in the United States very soon, judging from the new babies around my plant from seed and root division.

USED TO TREAT

Bronchitis

Colds

Cough

Fever

Gas

Headaches

High blood pressure

Infection

Pneumonia

Stomachache

USED AS/FOR

Anti-inflammatory

GROWING

The plant is found in some U.S. nurseries and is becoming more common. It can be grown from seed or by root division.

67

Medicinal Uses and Preparation

In its native Mexico this plant is known as a medicinal plant, and pharmacology tests have shown it has ingredients that are effective against a multitude of health problems.

I have used the flowers and leaves in a first-aid ointment for several years, and it works very well. It would probably work topically on inflammations or local infections such as boils if used as a poultice. Ordinarily, it is prepared as a tea or even a tincture using the above-ground parts of the plant.

It is used for headaches, stomach or intestinal problems, bronchitis, fevers, colds, coughs, gas, pneumonia, and to lower blood pressure.

Current Interest

Copper canyon marigold is antibiotic, anti-inflammatory, antispasmodic, and antibacterial.

Caution

Copper canyon marigold can cause a hypersensitivity to light and dermatitis. The leaves contain tannin, resin acids, and volatile oil. This plant should be approached with caution.

COPPER CANYON MARIGOLD
FIRST-AID SALVE

1 cup chopped copper canyon marigold or ½ cup of the dried
    herb (use any part but the root)
½ cup vegetable shortening

Melt the shortening in a pan. Stir in the herb. Set the pan into another pan containing boiling water (a double boiler will work fine). Leave uncovered for 1 hour, stirring occasionally. With fresh herbs, the ointment will keep only a short period. Ointment made with the dried herb will keep well.

Corn

Zea mays

Corn is, in all ways, a native plant of the Americas. It was a native grass very much like wheat that grew naturally. The Native American Indian developed corn as it is known today. The plant is held sacred among most of the North American tribes. Many groups use the pollen for special ceremonies, and it is believed to provide special powers. It is often carried in a special pouch to be used during prayers and is offered in the four directions. Some tribes use it during wedding ceremonies. There is a certain time when the Pueblo Indians have special ceremonial dances, in which the story of how corn was given to them is depicted. The Cherokees have a similar time in which the Green Corn Dance is done. In earlier times, the corn could not be eaten until the proper ceremonies had taken place.

Even the scientific name points to a plant set apart from others. The word *Zea* means "cause of life," and *mays* means "our mother."

USED TO TREAT
High blood pressure
Rheumatism
Warts
USED AS/FOR
Blood sugar regulation
Delivery of afterbirth
Diuretic
Food
Stimulant

Medicinal Uses and Preparation

Corn-silk tea is named in modern herbals as a diuretic and as a treatment for infection of the bladder. This is also a

GROWING

The corn stalk is grown from seed and must be cultivated. Usually it takes a fair-sized garden to produce a good quantity of corn for a family.

69

treatment used by many Native American Indian tribes. Fresh or dried corn silk can be made into tea. Low blood sugar, rheumatism, and high blood pressure are other conditions for which corn is used. It is also known as a stimulant. Salve is made from the smut, and smut is also used to aid in delivery of the afterbirth.* Silk and shuck poultices are often applied to boils.

Corn grains are used to remove warts, and they were also a common food for Indian braves on the trail, reputedly to increase lung capacity and help them continue on the journey.

Food

Mention corn, and the first thing many people think of is corn on the cob, or, as the country people say around east Texas, rosesneers. I had to interpret that for a doctor one day—roasting ears. There are whole cookbooks devoted to the culinary delights of corn.

The best tamales are wrapped in corn shucks. Wine has been made from corn, and of course moonshine, also known as corn licker, white lightening, or maybe "run-before-the-revenuers-catch-us."

There is an Indian corn soup called posole. Although it used to be made with an ash water or lime mixture, it can be made with what is in a modern kitchen.

To make posole: Wash one cup of shelled, dried corn, and add one tablespoon baking soda to it. Bring to a boil with water (enough to cover the corn, plus three inches more) in a stainless steel, iron, or glass pan with the lid on. Turn off the heat and let the corn sit overnight. Wash the kernels thoroughly, scrubbing off the skins. Repeat this until most of the shells are washed off. I scrubbed ten times the last time I made it. Cook in water until the corn is tender. You may add salt, chili powder, and pieces of pork or beef while it's cooking, but it's not necessary. Serve with flour tortillas baked on the grill or, better yet, serve with Indian fry bread.

Current Interest

Corn is used for urinary infections, as a diuretic, and to treat high blood pressure.

*Smut is the black powder found in chimneys after a fire is burned. Plants may have black growths that look like this powder (and hence are called smut). Smut is abnormal, a fungus. Rye plants may be infected with a type of smut that contains ergot and can make people sick.

HOT WATER CORNBREAD

1 cup cornmeal
¼ teaspoon salt
1 cup boiling water

Combine the meal and salt. Pour in the boiling water and stir quickly. Have a bowl with cool water to dip your hands in. Scoop out the dough and pat cakes between your fingers to a thickness of ¼ to ⅛ inch. Fry the patties in a thin layer of hot oil. Instead of oil, you may coat the pan with cooking spray, or you can bake the patties.

Note: The patties must have fingerprints on them or they will not be good.

THE MAKING OF CORNMEAL

In ancient days, a hole was hollowed out in solid rock near a riverbank. A stone that fit inside was found and the corn was ground with the stone. Another method was to grind the corn between stones. In some areas this is still practiced.

The Cherokees and other Indian tribes often used a hollowed-out section of tree trunk to make a deep cup. A pounding stick made of a smaller trunk was prepared, and corn was pounded with an up-and-down motion in the hollow trunk.

Later, mills were built near running water and stone wheels were moved across one another by the power of the water. The corn was ground between the stones. Today cornmeal is ground like flour, except that it is coarser. Many people still prefer stone-ground corn, however.

Cota   *Thelesperma megapotamicum*

In the mountains of New Mexico, cota, also called Indian tea or Navajo tea, can be seen along the roadsides with its small yellow bloom.

It is a slender little plant with very few stringy leaves and a small tuft of a flower with no petals. The stem may be branched several times, with one flower—if any—on each branch. The plant is green with a hint of blue.

Medicinal Uses and Preparation

The upper part of the plant can be dried in bundles, then stored for winter use.

According to Michael Moore in *Medicinal Plants of the Mountain West*, it is "a mild diuretic useful in water retention and urethra irritations . . . it is used for diaper rash and thrush when mixed with Malva . . ."

As with many herbal teas, cota tea is soothing and calming. Many claim it helps calm an upset stomach, and it has been used as a tonic for the blood.

Food

I hope this excellent tea will soon be discovered and will be generally available for those who have developed a taste for it. Many Native tribes of the Southwest use it as

USED TO TREAT

Diaper rash

Indigestion

Thrush

USED AS/FOR

Blood tonic

Diuretic

Sedative

Tea

GROWING

Cota is just beginning to be found in some specialized nurseries in west Texas and Utah.

a basic drink. The Navajo are especially fond of cota, and it was in Navajo territory that I got my first taste of Indian tea. (One taste was enough. Now when I travel into that area, I always return with a supply.) Even children drink it. The only caution that might be added is, as with all new foods and plants, watch for individual allergic reactions.

Current Interest

Cota is not a major plant as far as appearance, medicine, or food, but it is one of those little gems in a small package that is worth a try.

Caution

This is one of those nice plants that generally has no side effects.

COTA TEA

Gather two to three cota plants, without roots, put them together, and fold in four- to five-inch lengths evenly backward and then forward, then tie the bundle in the middle with a length of plant or string for drying.

Later, put one bundle of cota to one quart of water into a stainless steel pan and boil 5 minutes, then cover. Allow the tea to sit for 15 minutes, and serve. It has a golden color and a spicy fragrance.

Dandelion   *Taraxacum officinale*

Of all the herbs so far discussed, dandelion is one of the major ones. It is a plant found throughout the world and most cultures have found it useful. Its French name, *dent-de-lion* (lion's tooth, because of the toothed leaves), gives a clue to how the English name arose.

The long toothed leaves come directly from the brown root and form a basal rosette (the leaves grow in a circular pattern from the ground). Also from the root comes the hollow flower stem, which has no leaves and only a single yellow flower. This is one way to identify the plant. The flower stem is never branched. The flower later forms a puffy head made up of seeds, each with its own parachute. It seems children know instinctively just how to blow the fluff off a dandelion. All parts below the flower have a milky sap.

Medicinal Uses and Preparation

The whole plant can be dried for later use, and its effectiveness lasts up to a year. The upper portions may be laid across cheesecloth on a frame or on paper for drying. Either way, it is best to move them about occasionally while drying. The roots can be air dried or laid in an oven with only the pilot on. Roots of fresh spring plants can be made into tincture (use ten to thirty drops as needed), or tea may be made from the fresh leaves or roots. Tea may

USED TO TREAT

Anemia

Constipation

Corns

Heart trouble

Kidney stones

Rheumatism

Stomachache

Toothache

Warts

USED AS/FOR

Diuretic

Food

Liver purification

Spleen purification

Vitamins

GROWING

Dandelion plants may be bought or seeds can be planted. In some areas, dandelion is grown as a farm crop, the tops being used as greens.

74

also be made from the dried plant. The plant is rich in potassium, iron, phosphorus, and vitamins A, C, B, and D.

One of the main medicinal uses of dandelion is for the urinary tract. In Europe, China, and America it is used as a diuretic, to cleanse the kidneys and bladder, and as an anti-inflammatory in the treatment of rheumatism. The potassium content makes dandelion a safe choice as a diuretic because it would replace the potassium lost during diuresis. It is used by some to break up kidney stones and gravel.

The milk of the dandelion is used to remove warts and corns. It was a common treatment for toothache among some Indian tribes. If you are suffering from stress, a cup of dandelion tea may be just the thing to relax you or quiet an upset stomach.

Another widespread use is for cleansing and stimulating the spleen and liver. Even heart disease is among those problems treated with dandelion. Either eating the cooked leaves or drinking the tea is a treatment for anemia. The tea also acts as a tonic and stimulates digestion. For this reason, it acts as a mild laxative. Sliced raw root is effective on sores and inflammations of the mouth (Michael Moore, *Medicinal Plants of the Mountain West*).

Food

Dandelion has been used widely as a food. The roots are washed, peeled, and parboiled twice with a pinch of soda in the first boiling, and may be served with butter. The flowers can be boiled slightly, dipped in batter, and cooked as pancakes—served with syrup. The taproot can be boiled and pickled, or dried and used as a coffee-like beverage.

Current Interest

There is some evidence that dandelion relieves inflammation, whether for liver conditions or arthritis. This seems especially true with chronic conditions. "It has been reported that soy lecithin prevented cirrhosis in chimpanzees. Dandelion flowers were reportedly higher in lecithin than soy," James A. Duke writes in *Handbook of Edible Weeds*. Could this also be true with humans?

Other experiments have shown that dandelion might help in liver disorders, including gallstones. There is insulin in the roots.

Caution

Although dandelion is nontoxic, stomach upset may occur if it is eaten raw in large amounts.

 75

Desert Willow *Chilopsis linearis*

The desert willow, sometimes called the desert catalpa, has healing qualities that require no special preparation. It is a graceful tree, and its large purple blossoms are not only beautiful but heavily scented as well. It is a relaxant for anyone who stops a few minutes to enjoy the sight and scent.

USED TO TREAT

Cough

Fungus infection

Wounds

Yeast infection

USED AS/FOR

Antiseptic

Medicinal Uses and Preparation

The leaves can be prepared by lightly rinsing off any dust, toweling them dry, and placing the small limbs on a tray or paper so they receive plenty of air. They may then be stored in an airtight container and used on fresh wounds. Later, the leaves can be used for tea or can be powdered and used directly on minor wounds resulting in broken skin. The dried leaves will keep indefinitely. The bark and leaves can be tinctured and used in the same manner.

The flowers are more fragile. They must be dried carefully, perhaps on suspended cheesecloth, and the individual flowers must be turned often. They can be dried and used as a poultice for persistent coughs. They will retain their strength for about six months (Michael Moore, *Medicinal Plants of the Desert and Canyon West*).

GROWING

The tree is popular in landscaping and can be bought in nurseries.

Desert willow is effective against candida and other fungal infections. It is used after antibiotics or as a simple treatment for feminine itching. Make a basic tea and either drink it or use it as a douche for this problem (Michael Moore, *Medicinal Plants of the Desert and Canyon West*).

DESERT WILLOW TEA

2 teaspoons dried desert willow leaves
1 teaspoon dried, finely chopped *Echinacea* root
1 cup water

Heat water to near boiling. Place the leaves in a container and pour the water over them. Cover tightly and let stand for 30 minutes. Strain and keep the liquid covered in the refrigerator—it should not be used after 48 hours. Make up a new batch as needed.

The tea is good for yeast infections and other problems brought on by taking antibiotics. Take by sipping throughout the day, taking no more than 4 tablespoons in 24 hours. The tea can also be used as a douche for vaginal itching.

Devil's Claw   *Proboscidea*

My first impression of the devil's claw, also known as unicorn plant, was that it was some type of orchid. That idea was quickly pushed aside as I noted the dry dusty field, where no respectable orchid would be caught growing. The surroundings didn't seem to bother this tenacious little native, though. The leaves were big, about five by seven inches, and covered with tiny hairs. It was the flower that really stood out. It was pale lavender and about the size and shape of the small orchids often used in Hawaiian leis. The lower petal had streaks leading into the tube of the flower.

Later, at maturity, the pod, about six to eight inches long, splits open, and two curving hooks remain—the devil's claw. These frequently catch in the tails of horses and are the bane of farmers and ranchers. The plant is found in much of the United States.

Medicinal Uses and Preparation

The roots are used to treat the painful symptoms of arthritis. Devil's claw is considered by some a good liver tonic.

GROWING

The plants add a touch of the exotic to a garden, and they are easy to grow from seed. Seeds can be found in native-plant catalogs. Devil's claw has a reputation of being aggressive, but unwanted plants can be taken up easily.

Food

The seeds are eaten at any stage, but it is the green pods that are of real interest. The pods must be small, one-half to one and one-half inches long, to be prepared for eating. If they are any larger, they become bitter. They can be cooked in any way okra can, and the taste is similar. Try them boiled and buttered, rolled in cornmeal and fried, or put them into gumbo or soup as a thickening. They can also be pickled. In some areas of Mexico the leaves of the plant are cooked and eaten with beans, but I found them to be very bitter, even after parboiling.

The seeds are eaten in Mexico and the U.S. Southwest. Ripe seeds must be cracked and the meat taken out like a nut. The green ones can be eaten whole. They can also be toasted or ground into meal. They are high in protein, and an oil can be extracted from them. Some Indian tribes have used part of the root as food; others have eaten the boiled leaves (Delena Tull, *A Practical Guide to Edible and Useful Plants*).

Devil's claw has been used as a food crop in the United States and still is in Mexico and South America. The seeds are sold in some markets in Mexico.

Other Uses

The dried pods have been used in weaving baskets and also in some crafts.

Current Interest

Devil's claw has been the subject of laboratory studies involving animals that show its effectiveness as an anti-inflammatory. It is an analgesic and relaxes smooth muscles. Its action on the heart indicates it helps steady the heartbeat and lowers blood pressure. It was found in one study that devil's claw–root tea lowers fat and cholesterol levels. (Michael A. Weiner and Janet A. Weiner, *Herbs That Heal*).

STORAGE OF ROOTS

After the roots are dug up, they must be thoroughly cleaned. Shake off the dirt, then use a vegetable brush and clean under running water. Towel dry and remove rootlets. Cut the roots into thin slices and dry on paper or cloth. An oven with a pilot light makes a good drying chamber. When the root slices are thoroughly dry, seal them in a canning jar.

Dock

Rumex

One of the first plants seen in late winter to early spring is dock. Curly dock, or yellow dock, as some call it, is so named because of its long lance-shaped leaves that are slightly ruffled along the edges. It has bright yellow roots, which accounts for the second common name. The plant grows throughout the world, and there are numerous species.

Rumex species are frequently found in damp areas, but certain types grow on the dry western desert of the United States. Native American Indians of various tribes knew the value of the plant as a medicine, and it is interesting to find it being used for many of the same ailments among different cultures.

Medicinal Uses and Preparation

Wounds are treated with both the root and the leaves. The root may be pounded and applied as a poultice. In a similar manner, the leaves and stems have been used fresh or boiled, applied to injuries, sores, and boils. The plant is an astringent—it works to stop bleeding in minor wounds. Gather roots and leaves from plants that grow on dry soil. This should be done in winter or late fall.

Skin conditions have been treated with a decoction of the root made by boiling it in vinegar. An ointment

GROWING

This plant can be grown easily from seeds or roots. It has nice green leaves and the flowers are attractive in all stages. It must be kept well watered.

80

can be made by using a solid grease such as petroleum jelly, animal fat, or vegetable shortening (see instructions for making a salve on page 10). This is used to treat ringworm and other skin problems such as acne and ulcers.

The tea of dock leaf or root has been used for sore throats, rheumatism, and liver problems. It is also a treatment for burns and blisters, menstrual problems, dog bites, bug bites, anemia, hepatitis, venereal diseases, even tumors and cancers. According to the strength of the tea, it can stem diarrhea or act as a laxative.

Food

Because it has a high content of vitamins A and C, dock is very nutritious. The young leaves are good cooked as greens and should never be eaten raw. Sometimes, if the plant is a little bitter, it should be parboiled, washed, added to clear water, and cooked until tender. The seeds have been ground and made into flour.

Other Uses

The tannin content in dock is high enough for use in tanning leather.

Current Interest

Native American Indians who live in Arizona use dock for colds and sore throats.

Caution

The leaves contain oxalic acid, just as spinach does. Eaten in moderate amounts they are healthful; however, if very large amounts are eaten frequently, the oxalic acid can prevent the absorption of calcium.

DOCK FOR STINGING NETTLE

Dock is a well-known treatment for skin irritation caused by stinging nettle. The mashed dock leaves are rubbed on the affected part. If this fails, there is always the ancient British charm that is spoken while the dock is applied: "Nettle out, dock in, dock remove the nettle sting" (Inge Dobells, *Magic and Medicine of Plants*).

Dodder

Cuscuta

USED TO TREAT

Bruises

Constipation

Poison oak

Stinging nettle

Urinary tract
infection

USED AS/FOR

Anti-
inflammatory

Dye

Spleen
purification

If you are ever driving along and see a big wad of yellow or orange string lying across an area of several feet, you just might have found some dodder. It has aptly been described by Michael Moore as "claustrophobic mats of waxy, glistening yellow orange 'guts'." This plant is found in the southern portion of the United States as well as in other parts of the world.

Because of the way dodder holds plants, supporting them by wrapping and tightening, it is also called love vine. Dodder is in the morning glory family and grows from a seed, but that's where the similarity ends. As soon as the vine establishes itself on the host plants, its root withers and detaches, and the dodder begins taking nourishment from its neighbors. It has no leaves.

Medicinal Uses and Preparation

The vine may be pulled off other plants in a mat. Pick out the pieces of leaves and stems from the host plants. It is a good idea to rinse the dodder, blot it dry, and lay it out on paper to dry. Chop dried dodder for use in tea; store in an airtight container.

GROWING

Dodder is impractical, if not impossible, to grow. It kills any nearby plants.

The Cherokee used the plant for making poultices for bruises, and I've found this works well. It has also been used for kidney, liver, and spleen problems and swollen lymph nodes. The stem is a good laxative (Michael Moore, *Medicinal Plants of the Mountain West*).

Other Uses

There is no evidence that dodder was ever used as food, but the whole plant is a good dye. It produces a yellow color if alum is used as a mordant, orange if the mordant is tin.

Current Interest

In China, dodder has been found to be an anti-inflammatory and the seeds are used for urinary tract infections. It also has a quieting effect on the nervous system (Steven Foster and James A. Duke, *Eastern/Central Medicinal Plants*).

DODDER TEA

Use a rounded teaspoon of dried dodder in a cup of hot water. This makes a good laxative. If it is to be used for lymph node swellings, inflammation of the spleen, or liver problems, it should be taken in small amounts (½ tsp.) several times a day (Michael Moore, *Medicinal Plants of the Mountain West*).

Evening Primrose *Oenothera*

When the Old Ones of the Ani-Tsalagi tell the story of the beginning of the world, they speak of the two brothers who were made by the Father. These two brothers knew that people lived in the depths of the underground world in darkness and filth. The two descended down into the earth and led the people up. The sun was so bright that it made them cry, and the tears that fell grew into flowers of the sun, the evening primrose and sunflower.

The common or tall evening primrose can reach a height of six or seven feet. There are other similar primroses, but none as tall as this one. The leaves are thin and lance-shaped and the flowers are bright yellow. Evening primrose grows along ditches, creeks, and in the mountains. Seeds may be sown as an addition to any garden.

Medicinal Uses and Preparation

Not only has this plant had an active medical history, but its future is also extremely promising. It contains mucilage and is an astringent. This makes it ideal for a number of treatments. A decoction can be made of any part of the plant.

USED TO TREAT

Alcoholism

Arthritis

Asthma

Cough

Diabetes

Eczema

High blood pressure

Migraine

Premenstrual syndrome

Wounds

USED AS/FOR

Antiseptic

Astringent

Diuretic

Sedative

Weight loss

GROWING

Evening primrose is easily grown from seed, and plants may be bought in nurseries.

As an antispasmodic, evening primrose aids in calming coughs and asthma. It heals wounds and acts as an anti-inflammatory and has been used to reduce blood pressure. It is sometimes used as a diuretic and as a sedative. The root was used by early Indian tribes as a weight-loss aid.

Make a basic tea of roots or leaves. The recommended dosage is one to three teaspoons daily (Michael Moore, *Medicinal Plants of the Mountain West*).

Food

The plants have a large pink taproot that can be boiled. A first-year plant (before it flowers) is best used for food. The leaves can be boiled and seasoned for greens. If the plant tastes strong, parboil the leaves in one or two changes of water before serving.

Scrub and peel the large taproot. Boil in two changes of water, cook up to thirty minutes, season, and serve with butter. It can also be added to soups after boiling (Lee Allen Peterson, *Edible Wild Plants*).

Current Interest

Steven Foster and James A. Duke, in *Eastern/Central Medicinal Plants*, state: "Recent research suggests seed oil [of evening primrose] may be useful for atopic eczema, allergy induced eczema, asthma, migraines, inflammations, premenstrual syndrome, breast problems, metabolic disorders, diabetes, arthritis, and alcoholism."

In Britain, evening primrose is already an established treatment for premenstrual syndrome, and there are other possibilities for the future. Could it help hyperactivity, schizophrenia, parkinsonism, and anorexia nervosa? It is all possible, and research will tell.

Caution

Some people may be sensitive to the plant.

Flax

Linum

USED TO TREAT

Boils

Burns

Constipation

Cough

Eye infection

Gout

High cholesterol

Rheumatism

Scrapes

Skin infections

Sore throat

Stomachache

USED AS/FOR

Antiseptic

Cooking oil

Fiber

Food

Linen

History, whether fact or legend, is filled with the mention of flax. The Egyptians wrapped their dead in flax cloth. In the ancient Anasazi dwellings of Mesa Verde there are remnants of flax in the form of snares and twine. The Bible talks of linen as a basic for clothing. It was used by colonial settlers in America along with wool to produce linsey-woolsey for clothing. The plants are soaked in water to help decompose the fleshy parts. They are then dried and beaten to remove the fibers. They can then be spun and woven into linen.

Medicinal Uses and Preparation

The ripe seeds are the only part of flax that is used for medicine. The seed oil has many healing qualities. A flax-oil remedy for cancer of the skin and mouth was used by some Indians. Tea can also be made from the seeds. It has a soothing quality and can be used for stomach and intestine inflammations and kidney problems. Eating about one tablespoon of seeds with a large glass of water works as a mild laxative. In Early America, one seed was often put into an eye to aid in removing foreign bodies and to soothe at the same time.

GROWING

Flax can be grown from seed and will produce a thin-stemmed, lacy-leaved plant with bright violet-blue or gold flowers.

The high mucilage in an infusion of flax seeds is soothing to mucous membranes and aids in relieving the discomfort of a sore throat and cough. Seeds may be soaked in water and taken for stomach inflammation. Crushed seeds can be mixed with oil or water and applied to inflamed and swollen areas, boils, joints with gout or rheumatism, itching areas, burns, and old sores.

Food

The seeds can be boiled and eaten.

Current Interest

Flax seed oil has been found to be a healthy substitute for other cooking oil. It treats malnutrition and helps prevent blood clots in the veins. It has been used to help remove heavy metals (as in lead poison) from body tissues. It may also help reduce cholesterol in the blood.

Caution

All parts of the plant contain elements with a cyanide nature, i.e. cyanogenetic nitrates; unripe seeds are toxic (Claire Kowalchik and William H. Hylton, *Rodale's Illustrated Encyclopedia of Herbs*). Make sure flax seeds are ripe before using.

SOOTHING FLAX SYRUP

1/2 ounce flax seeds
1 cup water
1/4 teaspoon lemon or lime juice
2 teaspoons honey

Put the flax seed in the water. Soak until the mixture is thick, and add the juice and honey. Sip as needed for cough, sore throat, or stomach problems.

Fleabane *Erigeron*

The first impression of the fleabane is of a weedy plant. Looked at closely, however, the delicate flowers with their thin white petals are pretty little things—daisies for the little people.

There are several types of fleabane, two of which are Philadelphia fleabane (*E. philadelphicus*) and Canadian fleabane (*E. Canadensis*). These plants were used mostly by the Indians of North America and also by the early European settlers.

Medicinal Uses and Preparation

Basically, the fleabanes are all used alike. They are gathered while in bloom and dried in bundles or laid out on paper. The whole plant is generally used to make a tea or decoction. Fleabane is astringent and has been used for irritated mucous membranes, especially sore throats, colds, and stomach problems. It increases uterine contractions and brings on late menses.

Fleabane has been used by several Indian tribes for headache, as a diuretic, and for kidney problems, including kidney stones. The root was made into a decoction for heart problems. The whole plant was sometimes added to the stones in the sweat lodge.

USED TO TREAT

Congestion

Cough

Headache

Heart trouble

Kidney stones

Sore throat

Stomachache

USED AS/FOR

Diuretic

Insect repellent

Menstrual regulation

GROWING

Fleabane can be grown from seed.

Other Uses

As its name implies, fleabane smoke is supposed to get rid of fleas and gnats when the plant is burned.

Current Interest

Fleabane may be of use in stopping internal bleeding.

Caution

Fleabane should not be used during pregnancy.

FLEABANE FLOWERS

The flowers of fleabane have been used by different tribes of Indians in a number of different ways. They have been dried and made into a type of snuff to treat inflammation of the nasal passages and for headache. Other tribes used it to clear congestion from the head by sneezing. A tea for headaches made from the flowers of fleabane was supposed to be effective.

Garlic   *Allium*

USED TO TREAT

Acne
Arteriosclerosis
Asthma
Bronchitis
Candida
Cholera
Colic
Diarrhea
Dropsy
Dysentery
Gas
Gout
High cholesterol
Parasites
Salmonella
Scurvy
Shortness of
breath
Snakebite
Sore throat
Staphylococcus
Stomachache
Typhoid fever
Typhus

USED AS/FOR

Antibiotic
Antiseptic
Antispasmodic
Blood
purification
Blood sugar
regulation
Blood thinner
Diuretic
Expectorant
Food seasoning
Vitamins

In most places in the world there grows a plant that provides treatment for a multitude of ills and is well known by good cooks. Garlic contains many minerals and is rich in vitamins A, B$_1$, and C. Many bulbs that are sold commercially are much bigger than our natives. Garlic is one of the best-known seasonings, along with its cousin, the onion. Wild garlic is stronger than cultivated varieties and is possibly of more medicinal benefit.

Garlic is found in damp areas or places that have recently had rain. Look near creeks, rivers, or lakes. Garlic has a distinctive odor. Many find the odor overpowering, and perhaps this is the reason garlic has been used in numerous cultures as a charm against evil. Remember the vampire tales?

Medicinal Uses and Preparation

The bulb is the part used medicinally, and it may be made into a tea, syrup, or tincture. Fresh garlic is more effective than garlic that has been cooked or exposed to air. Whole garlic is of no medicinal use, but when it is crushed a chemical reaction occurs, and it becomes active and may be used as a medicine. It then deteriorates rapidly (Michael A. Weiner and Janet A. Weiner, *Herbs That Heal*).

Garlic has been used for centuries to give people strength. It was used specifically for wounds, even being

GROWING

Garlic may be grown easily from bulbs or young plants, which are available at most nurseries.

used in earlier days by soldiers in the field. Its use for infections was and is far-reaching—across the centuries and across continents. It has been shown in the laboratory to be a good antiseptic and antibiotic that is effective against candida, cholera, staphylococcus, salmonella, dysentery, and typhus. Garlic was used in ancient times for some of the same conditions.

Garlic works as an antispasmodic and expectorant, aiding in the relief of bronchitis, asthma, sore throats, and other respiratory problems. Colic, gas pains, diarrhea, and problems of the stomach and intestines may benefit from the use of garlic, as may the liver and gallbladder. It has even been used for scurvy, typhoid fever, and as a treatment for worms. Arteriosclerosis and gout are reputed to be relieved by garlic.

Externally, it is used on ringworm and acne. Native American Indians crushed the plant to use on snakebites.

Food

Garlic is eaten daily by millions of people. Check any recipe book—the culinary usage is endless.

Current Interest

Garlic has been the focus of many lab tests, and most current garlic treatments are not the result of random claims. Garlic has been used to improve circulation, as a diuretic, for shortness of breath, for dropsy (congestive heart failure), to thin the blood, to decrease blood sugar levels, to purify blood, to lower cholesterol and triglycerides and increase "good" cholesterol (HDL), and to protect the liver from drugs and pollution. There is also evidence that there may be help against several types of cancer hiding in garlic bulbs.

Caution

Some people may develop a rash from handling fresh garlic.

CROW POISON

Crow poison, or false garlic, is sometimes mistaken for onions or garlic. It has the same thin-bladed leaves, and even the flowers may look similar, but there is one very obvious difference: There is no odor of garlic or onion—and it is extremely poisonous.

Be sure the *Allium* you pull to eat smells. Usually both wild garlic and onion have a strong characteristic odor.

91

Gay-feather

Liatris

Tall purple-topped plumes with stiff narrow leaves of dusty green mark the gay-feather, which, singularly or in colonies, provides a spectacular show throughout most of the United States. Up close, the stiff columns look very much like fancy bottle brushes. Other species have broader leaves and many button-like tufts along the stems.

Medicinal Uses and Preparation

The Cherokee use the roots for backaches, pain in limbs, and as a diuretic (Paul B. Hamel and Mary U. Chiltoskey, *Cherokee Plants—Their Uses: A 400-Year-Old History*). It is also used for congestive heart failure, gonorrhea, and painful menstruation. In Mexico, small roots are burned and inhaled for headache and nosebleed. The smoke is also blown into a patient's throat for tonsillitis (Michael Moore, *Medicinal Plants of the Mountain West*). The root is valued as a treatment for bladder infections.

Other Uses

Native peoples of the United States and Mexico sometimes use the root as a talisman against witchcraft, evil spells, and snakes. The root is cut in two and one of the halves is carved into a cross, then both halves are worn

USED TO TREAT

Backache

Cough

Gonorrhea

Headache

Nosebleed

Snakebite

Tonsillitis

USED AS/FOR

Diuretic

Menstrual regulation

Talisman

GROWING

It's no wonder that gay-feather has now appeared in nurseries and florists' bouquets. It is attractive in the garden, long lasting as a cut flower, and stays pretty in dried arrangements. There are several species of *Liatris* with a number of common names: button snakeroot, snake master, and blazing-star, to name a few.

for protection. Babies, according to belief, are thought to be especially vulnerable to *mal de ojo* (evil eye).

Current Interest

One species of the plant has anticancer properties.

Caution

Another species, *L. odoratissima*, commonly called the vanilla plant, contains coumarin, a substance that prevents blood clotting. Care should be taken with it. Pregnant women should not ingest this substance, nor should anyone taking blood thinners.

GAY-FEATHER COUGH SYRUP

1/2 cup fresh gay-feather roots
1 cup cold water
1/2 cup honey

Clean and chop the roots. Put them in a pan with the cold water, cover, and bring to a boil. Turn the heat down and simmer for 20 minutes. Strain and return the liquid to the pan and simmer for 10 more minutes. Bottle and seal the syrup and store it in a cool dark place.

Goats' Head   *Tribulus terrestris*

Terror of the earth and puncture vine are two common names that truly describe the goats' head. The little vinelike plant is not noticed until a person or object comes in contact with the thorns (or horns). Generally, the plant's color is gray-green with small yellow petaled flowers that turn into a group of capsules containing seed. When broken apart, the individual pod looks like a goats' head, horns and all. The horns are straight and sharp enough to puncture small tires and big feet. The experience of stepping on them is very painful, and animals are often victims.

USED TO TREAT

Arteriosclerosis

Atherosclerosis

High blood
pressure

High cholesterol

Heart trouble

USED AS/FOR

Diuretic

Medicinal Uses and Preparation

Goats' head should be gathered after the fruit is in place and still green. Dry it, powder it, and make it into a tea to be taken twice a day, morning and night.

Goats' head is a strong medicine that helps to treat hardening of the arteries by cleaning out cholesterol, thus decreasing blood pressure. It is used to treat mild heart disease by an action similar to that of digitalis—strengthening the heart beat and slowing it—and at the same time it acts as a diuretic. The leaves and stems can also be dried and used, but they are not as strong as the heads.

GROWING

This is not a plant you would want to grow in your garden, and it is not necessary to grow it, because goats' head is quite prolific in untended waste spaces.

Current Interest

According to Michael Moore, extensive studies have shown that the seeds, and plant to a lesser degree, is a useful early treatment for elevated blood fats and cholesterols. It helps prevent or lessen the severity of arteriosclerosis and atherosclerosis.

Caution

Do not use goats' head when serious heart, kidney, or liver diseases exist. Do not use more than advised (Michael Moore, *Medicinal Plants of Desert and Canyon West*).

Goldenrod   *Solidago*

There are few who don't recognize the heavy nodding head of a goldenrod in bloom. A true native of the Americas, this plant has been the subject of art and poetry through the years. Goldenrod patterns on dishes, textiles, and in paintings bear witness to the popularity of this golden beauty, but its attraction goes beyond this.

Medicinal Uses and Preparation

Goldenrod is known in many countries as a medicinal plant, and both the Native American Indians and the European settlers knew its healing ways. The whole plant may be dried, but it should be picked while the flowers are young, or they will dry into a fluff. The roots are boiled and made into a decoction to treat colds, chest pain, fever, and liver problems. A piece of the chewed plant laid against a tooth is an old treatment for toothache. Topically, a root poultice has been made for application to boils, burns, rheumatism, neuralgia, and headaches.

Flowers are made into tea to treat sore throat, snakebite, fever, kidney and bladder problems, and as a laxative.

Washed and boiled leaves can be applied to wounds and sores. A tea made from the leaves is used as a blood

GROWING
Goldenrod plants grow well from seeds or roots, and they are popular as a border or background, for there are both tall and dwarf varieties.

96

tonic; to relieve gas pains, cramps, and colic; for colds, diarrhea, measles, coughs, and asthma.

The upper parts of the plant—the parts growing above the ground (often referred to as aerial parts)—are burned in the presence of the patient. This reportedly dries up congestion in the throat and is used to revive one from fainting. The tea, made from the flowers and leaves (sometimes even the root), is used for headaches, as an expectorant, an antispasmodic, an anti-inflammatory, and to cause sweating. It is a diuretic and may be used for bladder and kidney problems.

Food

The leaves and flowers of the sweet goldenrod (*S. odora*) make good tea and jelly. And recently, a Cherokee woman told me she loved goldenrod tea made from the root; she drinks it all the time.

Other Uses

The flower heads can be used to dye fabric, producing shades of yellow.

Current Interest

Goldenrod tea is good to take with other medicine for a urinary tract infection.

Caution

Some sensitive people may be allergic to goldenrod; however, the pollen is not airborne, as previously thought, rather pollination is accomplished by insects. Usually, it is ragweed, which grows in the same areas as goldenrod, that causes hay fever.

GOLDENROD SALVE FOR STINGS

1 cup goldenrod flowers, chopped
½ cup shortening

In the top part of a double boiler, heat the shortening until it is melted. Stir in the chopped flowers and cook in this manner for 45 minutes. Pour into a container to cool. The salve will keep better if it is stored in the refrigerator.

Grape

Vitis

USED TO TREAT

Arthritis

Anemia

Diabetes

Diarrhea

Fever

Headaches

Snakebite

Sore breasts

Stomachache

Thrush

Urinary tract
infection

USED AS/FOR

Anti-
inflammatory

Antiseptic

Beverage

Blood
purification

Food

If one plant were chosen as the best known throughout the world, the grape probably would win the contest. Throughout history, grapes or their products are spoken of. The presence of grapes in a land was a symbol of prosperity and fertility. Early Norse explorers of North America spoke of our country as "Vineland."

In the Bible, when Moses sent Joshua and Caleb to scout out a new land, they brought back huge bunches of grapes as evidence of a land worth going into. Wine, made from the grape, has been used in a number of religious practices, including those of the ancient Greeks and Romans. It is also used in the Christian practice of communion.

Medicinal Uses and Preparation

Although wine is mostly thought of as a beverage, it has many medicinal qualities. Wine with water, or water with wine, according to individual preference, is drunk in many parts of the world. Perhaps without knowing it, many imbibers have purified their water in this manner, thus preventing diseases. Wine has been taken as a tonic and a blood cleanser. Though it would not be my first

GROWING

Grape is usually grown from cuttings, roots, or small plants, but wherever the seeds fall a plant may grow. Grapevines can be bought in nurseries, and the whole personality of a yard can be changed by adding a grape arbor.

choice, wine would do as a makeshift wound or skin cleanser. It might be sticky, but wine is a good antiseptic substitute due to the alcohol it contains.

The sap of the grapevine has been used by both Europeans and Native American Indians as a treatment for eye problems. Here is an instance where two disparate cultures, without contact, use a plant for similar purposes. Grape leaf tea has been used in a number of countries for diarrhea, urinary infections, liver and stomach problems, thrush, headaches, and fevers.

Native American Indians used the grape plant in a number of ways other than those already mentioned. It was used in childbirth, and the leaves were used for sore breasts afterward. Snakebite was treated with the tendrils and ends of the vine. The vine itself was once used against certain poisons and to treat anemia. The roots made into tea were given for arthritis and diabetes.

Some health centers in Europe had what was called "grape cures." People were allowed to eat only grapes, and claims were made that this helped the kidneys and bowels. Results confirmed the grape to be a good way to maintain health (Nelson Coon, *An American Herbal Using Plants for Healing*).

Food

The fruit of the grapevine may be dried into raisins, eaten fresh, or enjoyed as a drink of either juice or wine. The fruit is used in many recipes. Even the leaf is used to wrap meat before cooking to add flavor and tenderize. Cream of tartar is made from the solid part of grapes, after the juice has been extracted.

Current Interest

The chewed seeds of the grape may have some activity against cancer (Reader's Digest, *Magic and Medicine of Plants*).

Research shows that ingredients in grape seed can help improve and protect against some degenerative diseases caused by exposure to environmental pollutants. In another test it was found that there was increased resistance to light glare in those who were given an extract from the grape seed.

When used in cosmetics, grape seed was found to be anti-inflammatory and to protect the skin from solar radiation (Ginger Webb, *Benefits of Grape Seed Extract*).

A similar vine is Canada moonseed (*Menispermum canadense*). Moonseed has a history as a medicinal plant and was used as a substitute for sarsaparilla; it was known as Texas sarsaparilla. The leaves are smooth rather than toothed, like the grape's leaves, and the fruit of this plant can be mistaken for grapes. But take caution: they are poisonous and can cause death.

TO BRING ON A WARM SPELL

If the weather is too cold for your taste, this can soon be remedied, according to these old Cherokee instructions. Make a fire using summer grapevines and post oak. This is bound to change even the coldest spell to a warm one (James Mooney, *James Mooney's History, Myths and Sacred Formulas of the Cherokees*).

Holly

Ilex

American holly, *I. opaca*, is one of the most common holly plants in the United States. In the South there is another holly, yaupon (*I. vomitoria*). Both are evergreen, and the American holly has a deeply toothed leaf with prickles on the end. Yaupon has an oval leaf with fine teeth on the edges. Both are attractive, especially when the bright red berries are visible.

Medicinal Uses and Preparation

The holly plant has been used in the United States throughout its history. The Indians used it for colic and indigestion. They also scratched the skin over cramped muscles with leaves (Paul B. Hamel and Mary U. Chiltoskey, *Cherokee Plants—Their Uses: A 400-Year-Old History*).

A treatment for inflammation of mucous membranes, gout, and pleurisy has been made from holly.

Yaupon was called the black drink plant and was made into a strong tea by many Indian tribes for the purpose of inducing vomiting. This tea was also a stimulant and was used as a purification before ceremonies. Yaupon tea decreases fever and causes sweating.

USED TO TREAT
Colic
Cramps
Fever
Gout
Indigestion
Pleurisy

USED AS/FOR
Anti-inflammatory
Diaphoretic
Emetic
Stimulant
Tea

GROWING
Hollies may be obtained from most nurseries.

101

Food

The leaf of both types of hollies can be made into an enjoyable beverage tea (Euell Gibbons, *Stalking the Healthful Herbs*).

Current Interest

The leaves can be used as an emetic to treat poisoning.

Caution

The berries are toxic, although up to ten of them can be taken as an emetic.

HOLLY TEA

1 teaspoon prepared, broken holly leaves (yaupon is very good)
1 cup hot water

Preparing the leaves: Place the leaves in an oven or in an iron skillet. Dry the leaves, then cook them until they are deep brown.

Break the prepared leaves and steep them in the hot water for 10 minutes.

If it is to be used as an emetic, increase the measurement of leaves to 2 teaspoons.

Honeysuckle   *Lonicera japonica*

Children can be some of the best judges of flowers because all of their senses are not yet cluttered with responsibility. The important thing to them is to enjoy the flowers, whether that be to smell them, blow dandelion puffs, or suck the nectar from a honeysuckle.

Honeysuckle is a plant loved by many. Because its sweet aroma has a relaxing quality, it is often planted around porches, where its odor can be enjoyed at the end of the day.

Japanese honeysuckle, *L. japonica*, is the best known species, and although not native, it has naturalized itself in much of the United States—so much so that it has become a pesky weed to many people.

Medicinal Uses and Preparation

As a medicinal plant, honeysuckle is used in a tea made from the fresh or dried flowers or stems. To dry properly, the flowers must be spread out in a dry place with plenty of ventilation. One quick and easy method is to place them on newspaper in an oven with a pilot light. The leaves and stems can be dried in the same way.

Honeysuckle tea has been used for gastrointestinal infections and pain. It is beneficial when given for laryngitis,

USED TO TREAT

Asthma
Boils
Constipation
Cough
Fever
Flu
Food poisoning
Gonorrhea
High blood pressure
High cholesterol
Kidney stones
Laryngitis
Swollen glands
Scabies
Tumors
Yeast infection

USED AS/FOR

Blood sugar regulation
Diuretic
Menstrual regulation
Tea

GROWING

Plants can be bought at nurseries, or if you have a friend who will share, just pull some up by the roots and plant them. Honeysuckle is very invasive but makes a beautiful climbing vine on a fence or arbor.

 103

colds, fever, and flu. Honeysuckle is antispasmodic and anti-inflammatory. Externally, a double-strength tea is used as a poultice on boils and tumors and is applied to skin for scabies.

Native American Indians use another species, *L. dioica*, for medicine. A tea is made of the bark and used for constipation, painful menstruation, kidney stones, yeast infection, gonorrhea, and as a diuretic.

Food

A glass of iced tea can be flavored with the flowers, or a hot tea can be made from the leaves, stems, or flowers. It might be interesting to try the flower in certain foods, as is done with roses.

Current Interest

Laboratory tests have proven *L. japonica* is effective in lowering blood pressure and cholesterol. It also lowers or raises blood sugar. It has antibacterial and antiviral qualities and is therefore helpful in the treatment of laryngitis, boils, and swollen glands. It also treats food poisoning.

Caution

Do not use the berries—they are poisonous.

HONEYSUCKLE ASTHMA AND COUGH SYRUP

1 tablespoon fresh (or 1 rounded teaspoon dried) honeysuckle flowers
1 tablespoon fresh (or 1 rounded teaspoon dried) mullein leaves
2 cups honey

Put all ingredients in a pan. Bring to a boil over low heat. Turn the heat very low and simmer slowly for 20 minutes. Strain, and pour the syrup into a sterile bottle. Keep in a dark and cool place. Take 1 teaspoonful as needed.

Hop Tree *Ptelea trifoliata*

A gentle wind rises and touches the branches of the hop tree, releasing a soft sigh. Its song is a quiet *shhhh*, much like distant rain, as the fruit brush together. This attractive tree is small but well worth growing. It is also called wafer ash and swamp dogwood. The leaves cluster in threes and are sage green. The fruit hang together, looking like large clusters of rolled oats with a seed in the middle and an encircling wing. The flavor is very bitter.

USED TO TREAT
Asthma
Fever
Gout
Parasite
Rheumatism
Stomachache

USED AS/FOR
Anti-inflammatory
Appetite stimulant

Medicinal Uses and Preparation

The bark can be boiled and used for fever, gout, rheumatism, and has even been taken to enhance the effectiveness of other medicines. It is used as a tonic to stimulate appetite and for stomach upsets. The bark and roots have been used in place of quinine. The leaves are made into a bitter tonic that is used for the treatment of worms and asthma. The fruit is also tonic, and in spite of its bitter taste is reportedly good for severe stomach upsets and inflammation of the intestinal tract.

Caution

Don't use hop tree to medicate children, because it might cause vomiting. Because hop trees have three leaflets, as

GROWING

The tree is cold-tolerant and can be bought in nurseries or grown from seed. It is usually about fifteen feet tall or a little taller and is very attractive in the summer and fall because of its fruit. The tree is scattered throughout much of the United States.

 105

does poison oak, care should be taken with identification. Look at the whole tree. Poison oak, being a vine, has been known to climb on tree limbs, giving rise to confusion.

WHERE THERE'S A WILL

Early American settlers, who were used to having their beer, were feeling the loss as they moved west. Desperate, they began to look for something that would take the place of the European hops they were used to. Maybe the fruit of the hop tree caught someone's eye and he was reminded of the hop vine of the Old World. However it happened, a passable brew was concocted from the hop tree. Thus the little tree, previously the wafer ash, got its new name.

Horehound   *Marrubium vulgare*

Horehound was always in our yard when I was a little girl. My grandmother had a big bush, and we depended on it for cough medicine. For awhile after I grew up it could only be found growing around old deserted farmhouses, but with the resurgence of interest in traditional medicine, it now grows in fields, along roadsides, and in parks throughout the United States.

Medicinal Uses and Preparation

When a cough has gotten steadily worse, with congestion, it is time to reach for the horehound. It can be made into a syrup, a decoction, or candy, all of which are effective in loosening phlegm. Horehound is best known for its use in the treatment of respiratory problems such as bronchitis and tuberculosis. Because it is a bitter herb, it works as a tonic, and a decoction may be used for this. Add a little honey to make it more tasty.

    Horehound is also used as a diaphoretic and may decrease the fever of colds, flu, or typhoid fever. It is said to soothe sore throats, aid skin problems, and decrease menstrual pain. Use it as a vermifuge to get rid of worms and as an insect repellent.

    Because horehound is used as a calming medicine with a sedative effect, it has been used in cases of heart

USED TO TREAT
Bronchitis
Congestion
Cough
Fever
Hepatitis
Malaria
Menstrual pain
Parasites
Skin problems
Sore throat
Stomachache
Tuberculosis

USED AS/FOR
Beer brewing
Insect repellent
Muscle relaxant
Sedative

GROWING

Horehound is still good in gardens with its dusty wrinkled leaves with silver beneath and its bundles of flowers up the square furry stem. The flowers are not outstanding, but the plant makes a good contrast to more showy herbs. It can be started from seed or transplanted.

 107

problems (probably the types brought on by anxiety, rather than heart disease) and is described as a muscle relaxant. It is a stimulant and used for stomach and gallbladder problems and hepatitis.

Horehound has been put to work to treat malaria when quinine is unavailable. It is given after childbirth in some cultures, including that of Native American Indians.

Food

Horehound can be substituted for hops in brewing beer.

Horehound definitely is an acquired taste, and those who have eaten it all their lives find it quite tasty; however, an older child or adult who is new to it may find it unpleasant.

Current Interest

Although horehound is an old-time medicine, it can be found in most drugstores as cough drops today.

Caution

If used regularly over a long period of time, horehound can cause hypertension in some cases—possibly in those with a preexisting inclination.

HOREHOUND CANDY COUGH DROPS

2 cups sugar
1 cup water
1 small handful (about 3 tablespoons) horehound leaves and
    stems

Boil the horehound leaves in the water for 5 minutes. Cover, and remove from the heat. Let sit for 5 minutes, then strain and discard the solids. Add the sugar to the liquid and bring to a boil. Cook to a hard-crack stage, then pour into a well-greased platter.

Loosen the edges while the candy is cooling. Break into small pieces and use as cough drops.

Horsetail

Equisetum

Horsetails existed with the dinosaurs during the Carboniferous period. It was then the main plant group in the world. There were many kinds, both large and small (Michael Moore, *Medicinal Plants of the Mountain West*).

Big masses of horsetail grow near water or in boggy areas. The tall green type is that which is used medicinally.

Medicinal Uses and Preparation

The green stalks may be cut near the ground and tied in loose bunches. They should then be hung to dry; make sure they have plenty of dry air and circulation.

The tea may be used both internally and externally. It is used for urinary tract infections or inflammation, bed-wetting, swelling from water in the tissues, and as a blood tonic. It also helps repair damaged tissues. Other uses are for arthritis, ulcers, and eczema. It also decreases bleeding, both internally and externally.

Some Native American Indians use horsetail to treat kidney and bladder ailments. Others use it for healing wounds by poulticing.

USED TO TREAT

Bed-wetting

Eczema

Stomach ulcer

Urinary tract infection

USED AS/FOR

Anti-inflammatory

Astringent

Blood tonic

Calcium

Dye

Forming collagen

GROWING

Horsetail is another of those plants that does better in the wild because of its specialized environmental requirements. But should you have a source of standing water, you could grow it. It can be grown on the edge of a lily pond in which the water is slow-moving or still.

Food

The heads of the plant may be eaten. For this they should be boiled, or they could be pickled (Lesley Bremness, *Herbs*).

Other Uses

Horsetail is used on fine furniture to sand the finish. It works like steel wool. Horsetail can also yield a yellow dye.

Current Interest

Horsetail has a high silica content that is readily absorbable. Because of this, it aids in the development of bone and helps with collagen formation. These are areas in which women in menopause have problems, and drinking horsetail tea should benefit weakening bones and help prevent fractures and degeneration. The plant also contains calcium and other minerals that can be a big help in rebuilding damaged tissues. The tea may also help in the treatment of stomach ulcers (Michael A. Weiner and Janet A. Weiner, *Herbs That Heal*).

Caution

The tea should be taken in small amounts for no more than three days to prevent toxicity.

Don't collect horsetail in areas that might contact runoff from fertilized fields. These plants could contain toxins.

PAN SCRUBBER OF HORSETAIL

Make a bundle of horsetail about six to seven inches in length. Tie it tightly in three places, and trim the ends evenly. This works well as a substitute for steel wool.

Indigo

Baptisia

The first thing that catches the eye when someone first sees wild indigo is the blossom, which looks very much like a bunch of cream-colored grapes hanging very low on the plant. Often one end is lying on the ground. Indigo looks very much like wisteria with no vine. The individual flowers are similar to those of peas. The leaf is divided into three leaflets.

Medicinal Uses and Preparation

An ointment has been made from the seeds and rubbed on the stomach for colic. The root tea was once used for typhoid fever, scarlet fever, and malaria. It was also a treatment for colitis and dysentery. A weak tea can be used to treat nausea.

The leaves and stems have been made into a decoction that was used as a stimulant to treat snakebite. The plant is an astringent and antiseptic, making it a good treatment for wounds and sores.

Native American Indians used the plant for snakebite, sores, and for skin problems.

Other Uses

The roots can be boiled and used as a blue dye.

USED TO TREAT
Colic
Colitis
Dysentery
Malaria
Nausea
Scarlet fever
Skin problems
Snakebite
Sores
Typhoid fever
Wounds

USED AS/FOR
Antiemetic
Antiseptic
Astringent
Stimulant

GROWING
The attractive indigo may be grown from seed.

There is some evidence that indigo can boost the immune system.

Indigo may be toxic.

INDIGO TEA TO STOP VOMITING

Make a basic tea from indigo roots. Let this cool and add a few cubes of ice. Take sips to stop vomiting.

Jimsonweed   *Datura*

Some might call datura a mystical plant. Used all over the world, it often held people in awe, and sometimes in fear. A bit of extract in the wine of an enemy and there would be no more enemy. It is said by some to have been the force behind the oracle at Delphi. In the ancient days of North America, shamans used the plant to induce visions. It was used in ceremonies for the coming of age of young men in some tribes. Most of this use has been abandoned because of datura's dangerous side effects, which often include death.

USED TO TREAT
Asthma
Burns
Hemorrhoids
Joint aches
USED AS/FOR
Analgesic
Anti-inflammatory
Antispasmodic
Hypnotic
Narcotic
Sedative

Medicinal Uses and Preparation

Datura, also known as jimsonweed or thorn apple, contains an alkaloid called hyoscine whose effect is not reliable because there are differences in every plant determined by where the plant may be growing, among other factors. Even the ancient experts who used datura could not predict the outcome of using it—and many did not survive its effects.

That factor still remains, and even though datura is still claimed by some to be ideal for use in some internal treatments, it can't be emphasized enough: Do not take any part of this plant internally.

GROWING

This plant is frequently used in landscaping. The large trumpet-shaped flowers are white to deep purple, and some have double blossoms. The foliage is attractive with its lushness and big leaves. Care must be taken if it is grown where there are children, because handling the plant or ingesting the seeds or other parts can be deadly.

 113

Datura has been used as a narcotic, an antispasmodic, and for pain relief. It is a sedative, a hypnotic, and has been used to treat epilepsy.

Datura has been used for years as a treatment for asthma, wherein a pinch of dried leaf is dropped into a flame and the smoke inhaled. It is also smoked for the same purpose. This has been an effective treatment, and many use it. Datura poultices and ointments are an old remedy for swollen, painful joints, external hemorrhoids, and minor burns.

According to Michael Moore in *Medicinal Plants of the Mountain West,* "a cup of the chopped plant and a tablespoon of Cayenne Pepper steeped in a quart of rubbing alcohol for at least a week, makes a good analgesic liniment."

Tea made of the leaf can be made and poured into bathwater, but care must be taken, especially if the bather is elderly, not to stay in the tub long, because there is some absorption of the active ingredients of the plant into the system through the skin, and even more through the mucous membranes.

Current Interest

Several treatments using datura have proved to be valid but carry a real possibility of death or insanity.

Caution

This plant is extremely poisonous and should never be taken internally. Many young people have eaten datura with the intent to get high and have paid with their lives. This plant is not in the same league as marijuana or even peyote. Most people who have ingested datura have suffered serious poisoning. When poisoning occurs the pupils dilate, the face becomes flushed, the heartbeat is rapid, a dry mouth is present, and there is a feeling of impending doom. Then one falls into a coma and eventually dies.

HOW JIMSONWEED GOT ITS NAME

It was 1676 when British soldiers were sent to Jamestown, Virginia, to put down an uprising of the colonists. Food was short, and the large-leafed *datura* plants looked good—as if they would make a good potherb. The soldiers gathered the leaves and cooked them for greens. Those who ate the concoction began to hallucinate and continued to do so for eleven days.

Strangely, there were no deaths. Afterward the plant was called the Jamestown weed, later shortened to jimsonweed. Experts believe that cooking it may have weakened the poison. This is only a theory, however. Cooking did not prevent several teens from dying from drinking jimsonweed tea in El Paso, Texas, a few years ago.

Jujube

Ziziphus Jujuba

The jujube tree is native to China and has become naturalized in the United States. It likes to be near a stream; however, it may be found in some rather dry areas and seems to thrive when it is established. It is called "Chinese date" by many people.

Medicinal Uses and Preparation

The fruit of the jujube has been used for coughs, to rid the body of poisons, and for heart conditions. It is made into a cough drop for this purpose, and the seed may be given for anxiety, insomnia, and even dizziness. The bark has been used for diarrhea, and the root is given to relieve fever and make hair grow (Lesley Bremness, *Herbs*).

Food

Jujube fruit, which is about the size and shape of a date, is good when eaten fresh. It is similar to an apple in taste, though much drier. It can be dried or it can be candied and used as a date. The fruit has also been pickled. The inside of the hard pit is edible.

Current Interest

Research suggests jujube may promote immunity (Lesley Bremness, *Herbs*).

USED TO TREAT

Cough

Diarrhea

Dizziness

Fever

Heart trouble

Insomnia

USED AS/FOR

Food

Hair growth

Sedative

GROWING

Started trees may be bought at nurseries, and the seeds will grow easily.

CANDIED JUJUBES

1 cup jujube fruit
1 cup cool water
2 cups sugar
1 cup water

Cook the jujube fruit in 1 cup of water by bringing it to a boil and cooking for 3 minutes. Pour off the water and allow the fruit to sit.

Bring the 2 cups of sugar and 1 cup of water to a boil and cook to the soft-ball stage. Add the cooked jujube fruit and cook slowly until the mixture is clear and the fruit is tender. Drain the fruit. The candied jujube fruit can be placed in a glass jar and kept until ready to use in cakes, breads, candies, or for eating by themselves.

Juniper

Juniperus

This is the reason the juniper, often called cedar, is red, as told by the old men of the Yuchi and Cherokee peoples. In a day almost forgotten, there was an evil conjurer who kept interfering with the way of the sun on its journey across the sky. Finally he was found in his cave and killed. His head was cut off, but it refused to die. The people were told to hang it in the top of a tree, but each day the head still lived. It was moved from tree to tree with no success, until it was hung in the cedar tree. Here it died as the blood dripped down the trunk. The wood became red because of this. From then on, it was known as the "Medicine Tree."

The cedar is an important tree to the Cherokee. It had endured a task set for all trees, and because of this, it was allowed to keep its leaves during the winter as a mark of its fortitude. Three things make it notable: its green color, which lasts during the coldest of weather; its deep, pleasant smell; and its self-preservation (James Mooney, *James Mooney's History, Myths, and Sacred Formulas of the Cherokees*).

GROWING

Juniper can be transplanted from the wild—it is in no danger of extinction—or, for a good start, get a tree from a nursery.

Juniper leaves and berries are often carried as a protection against bad influences. The leaves are frequently used in ceremonies in the sweat lodge or as incense during certain observances. This special tree is widely used among Native American Indians throughout the United States.

Medicinal Uses and Preparation

Some of juniper's medical uses include: as treatment for coughs, colds, ulcers, wounds, boils, fever, venereal diseases, urinary infections, and as a diuretic.

Some of the same juniper treatments have been found in the records of ancient Egypt and in the folk medicine of Europe. Many of these treatments are still used by Native healers and herbalists.

Known mainly for use to treat bladder infections and as a diuretic, juniper is also used to stimulate stomach acid and relieve an upset stomach. One teaspoon of berries or leaves steeped in a cup of hot water may be sipped several times a day. Juniper also contains antiseptic properties, and the tea can be used as a wash to disinfect the skin. A few leaves or berries in water used as an inhalant seems to loosen congestion and relieve chest colds.

Although the essential oil of juniper can burn the skin, an infusion of juniper berries and small branches steeped in oil is one I've found safe and effective. It is used as a massage oil, a rub for sore muscles, in the bath for muscle and joint pain, or as an insect repellent.

Food

This versatile tree has been used as flavoring in gin and as a seasoning for meat or stews (ten berries per pound of meat—especially wild game).

Other Uses

The limbs, bark, and wood can be used as a dye. In a very concentrated bath of leaves and limbs, I got a rich russet color on cotton cloth. The wood of juniper is widely used because of its beauty, smell, and protection against insects, for instance, in a cedar chest.

According to Michael A. Weiner and Janet A. Weiner, in *Herbs That Heal*, in animal experiments juniper has been shown to have antitumor activity and to be antiviral in nature. Within cell culture it acts against the flu virus A2 and herpes simplex virus I and II and is also an in vitro antibacterial against several human pathogens. Studies also indicate its diuretic quality and its aid in the treatment of arthritis. The "Medicine Tree," with its wide popularity and use in treating various ills, is one of the major Native herbals.

Caution

Some authorities advise against the use of juniper. The United States Department of Agriculture considers it an unsafe herb. It can be toxic in large doses and when it is used over a long period of time. It should not be used where kidney problems exist or during pregnancy, because it is a uterine stimulant. Also, because many people are allergic to the pollen, extra care should be taken by those people when using juniper as a treatment.

INFUSED JUNIPER OIL

Use juniper branches with berries, if possible. Rinse off dust and towel the branches dry. Let them dry for twenty-four hours.

Pack a canning jar with the juniper. Pour hot vegetable oil over this until it is one-half inch over the top of the leaves.

Place in the dark for ten days, then strain the oil off into another jar. Let this sit for seven days, then gently pour off the oil into another jar, leaving any water that may be in the bottom of the first jar. This water will eventually cause the oil to spoil.

Store in a dark and cool place. This is used as a bath oil and a massage oil for sore muscles or joints. It is said to work well as an insect repellent.

Lamb's-quarters *Chenopodium*

How would you like to have fresh spinach from your yard much of the year? Lamb's-quarters tastes very much like spinach, with a mild flavor, and will start growing long before cold weather is gone and keeps on until the late fall or early winter. Although some of the older leaves may get tough, it never gets bitter. The name *Chenopodium*, or "goosefoot," is a clue to identifying the plant. The leaves remind one of the foot of a goose.

Medicinal Uses and Preparation

It should be used fresh or frozen. It prevents scurvy and has been used for stomachache and diarrhea. Topically, it has been applied as a poultice or a tea for burns and itching.

Food

The greens were enjoyed by Indians and settlers alike; they are still eaten by those who live close to the land—or those who remember this taste treat from childhood. Cook it like spinach and add a little butter. The seeds can be eaten, and Indian tribes have cooked them as a cereal. Settlers ground and added them to all types of breads. It has been found that the seeds are equal or superior to most grains in protein content.

USED TO TREAT
Burns
Calcium
Diarrhea
Itching
Scurvy
Stomachache
USED AS/FOR
Food
Vitamins

GROWING

Until recently, lamb's-quarters was not available in nurseries, but now not only the seeds but also the young plants can be purchased. Lamb's-quarters is usually looked on as a weed, but it can be a valuable plant to have in the garden. The plant growing in my garden has more purple than usual and is a good addition for its color. Lamb's-quarters is in the same goosefoot family as spinach, beets, and chard.

121

Current Interest

The young leaves and tops of plants have more nutrients than spinach. They are high in vitamins C and A and contain calcium.

Caution

Lamb's-quarters contains oxalic acid just as spinach does, and it binds calcium and prevents its absorption in the body. If your calcium levels are within normal limits or your intake is good, these greens should not affect you negatively. But eating them frequently or in large amounts is not recommended. Simply be moderate.

Some people are allergic to the pollen of this plant.

NOT NEW BUT OLD

Lamb's-quarters was once thought to be nonnative in North America, but archaeologists in Canada have discovered that the Blackfoot Indians used the seeds about A.D. 1500 (Delena Tull, *A Practical Guide to Useful and Edible Plants*).

Larkspur
Delphinium

In the spring, the violet blue of a larkspur may be the first color that dots the roadside or the edge of the woods. Years ago this flower was used medicinally, but today it is little used because there are other plants that are more effective and safer to use internally.

Medicinal Uses and Preparation

Today larkspur's only use is for lice, the itch of scabies, and crab lice. Michael Moore (*Medicinal Plants of the Mountain West*) suggests gathering seeds, buds, and flowers and making a tincture using one part ground seed and five parts alcohol, vinegar, or green soap (a liquid soap available in most drug stores). This must be mixed and allowed to steep about seven days before straining. The tincture of green soap works best in the hair. This is applied to wet hair and left on for ten minutes. The alcohol solution may be more effective on the skin for scabies. The vinegar solution may be used for crab lice. If irritation occurs, stop using the solution.

USED TO TREAT
Crab lice
Lice
Scabies

Caution

Do not use where there are sores, scratches, or when skin is badly irritated. The poison from the seeds can be absorbed through broken skin, and general sickness can occur. The plant is poisonous—do not take it internally.

GROWING

Larkspur is frequently used in gardens with pretty results. The seed can be planted in the fall for early-spring blossoms.

123

LARKSPUR VERMIN WASH FOR ANIMALS

Using the green soap solution with larkspur seed, wet the pet, work up a lather, and wait ten minutes. Rinse well.

Caution: If the pet has red areas that are scratched or open, do not shampoo—it could cause poisoning (Michael Moore, *Medicinal Plants of the Mountain West*).

Lemon Balm   *Melissa officinalis*

The sweet, tart smell of lemon flows out whenever a stem or leaf of lemon balm is crushed—who can resist? This plant has been a favorite through the years, and as immigrants came to the United States, the friendly herb moved with them. Brought from Europe, this little alien has become naturalized in the United States and grows in most areas. Like mint, it has a square stem and oval leaves that are rough and grow opposite each other. Its flowers are inconspicuous little white or yellow things, but its lemon scent and medicinal qualities make it a necessity in the medicine garden. When any part of the plant is crushed, its odor becomes evident.

Medicinal Uses and Preparation

The plant has been used through the centuries as a tonic for longevity and helps improve poor memory. Perhaps the smell is important to its healing benefits, because it is well known that a cup of lemon balm tea helps get rid of depression and nervousness. Its sedative and antispasmodic effects may play a role in relieving headache, indigestion, and sleeplessness. It is also a treatment for stomachache, colic, and nausea, and many claim it is beneficial in relieving painful or delayed menstruation, dizziness, asthma, and

USED TO TREAT

Asthma

Bronchitis

Colic

Depression

Diarrhea

Dizziness

Fever

Headache

Insomnia

Memory loss

Nausea

Nerves

Stomachache

USED AS/FOR

Antihistamine

Anti-inflammatory

Antiseptic

Antispasmodic

Bath oil

Food seasoning

Massage oil

Menstrual regulation

Sedative

GROWING

Lemon balm will grow easily from seed or roots.

125

bronchitis. The tea is also taken to reduce fever, for diarrhea, and as an antihistamine.

Other uses include applying a poultice of lemon balm on swollen joints caused by rheumatism and on tumors. Because it is an antiseptic, it helps alleviate some skin problems. It can be tinctured, and made into an ointment and tea. If the tea is to be used topically, it should be made with two teaspoons of dried herb (or two tablespoons fresh) in one cup of water.

Lemon balm also has antibacterial characteristics. A lemon balm oil massage is soothing and relieves tension. The fresh leaf is usually best, but the leaves and stems may be dried and used in the same way.

Food

Lemon balm tea is a pleasurable beverage, and it may be served hot or cold. Try the leaves in a fruit salad or on cooked meat. Even vegetables are good with lemon balm added. You are only limited by your own imagination. A cup of lemon balm tea at mealtime aids in digestion. It is good for making lemon-flavored vinegar.

Other Uses

Dried lemon balm is good in potpourri and for making sweet-dream pillows. The plant is used in perfume and cosmetics. Add leaves to bathwater for a relaxing bath. You might even have a cup of lemon balm tea (for a double whammy) while bathing.

Current Interest

Experiments have been done that show the extract of lemon balm in hot water is very effective as an antiviral in such diseases as herpes and mumps. It is also antihistaminic, antispasmodic, and antioxidant (Steven Foster and James A. Duke, *Eastern/Central Medicinal Plants*).

SWEET-DREAM PILLOWS

My little ones used to have bad dreams, and I decided to give things a little boost. I made them little pillows about two inches square and filled them with a bit of cotton and something that smelled sweet. Lemon balm is a good pillow stuffing. I never heard a word from the kids after giving them the pillows and found them asleep, clutching the pillows near their noses.

Lemongrass   *Cymbopogon citratus*

Tall waving bunches of bright green blades are characteristic of lemongrass. Its smell is not as strong as lemon balm, but its flavor is lasting. This plant is found throughout Mexico and along the U.S. border and is used in teas and for medicines.

Medicinal Uses and Preparation

Tea can be made and applied topically to acne, as an antiseptic, and for athlete's foot. It is also used for diarrhea, stomachache, fevers, and flu. A cup of the tea in a quiet situation could assist in getting rid of a headache because it has both sedative and analgesic qualities. For an invigorating bath, add strong tea to the water before bathing.

Food

Lemongrass has been used as a food coloring and for lemon flavoring. It is very good as a tea, both by itself or mixed with other flavors.

Current Interest

Lemongrass contains a substance that may be helpful in reducing mutations during the formation of human embryos. It has proven active against *Escherichia coli*, a

USED TO TREAT
Acne
Athlete's foot
Diarrhea
Fever
Flu
Headache
Stomachache
USED AS/FOR
Analgesic
Antiseptic
Bath oil
Sedative

GROWING

Lemongrass's popularity does not stop with its medicinal use but continues to the garden, where it is an attractive herb. Most nurseries have lemongrass in stock in the spring. It grows in bunches, like multiplying onions, and stalks with roots can be transplanted. Frequently it can be found in grocery stores, especially Oriental stores. Check the root section; it only takes a small root to grow.

 127

frequent cause of food poison and infections, and *Staphylococcus aureus* (Michael A. Weiner and Janet A. Weiner, *Herbs That Heal*).

LEMON AND MINT TEA

½ teaspoon chopped lemongrass
½ teaspoon crushed mint (your favorite kind)

Place the herbs in a tea ball or spoon and place in a cup. Fill the cup with hot water, cover, and let the tea steep for 10 minutes. Take for headache, relaxation, or just to enjoy. This can also be made into an iced tea.

Licorice

Glycyrrhiza

Long black licorice whips may be the first thing that comes to mind when we think of licorice. But long before we had that confection, children were given the small dried roots of wild licorice to chew on. The roots are very sweet and many people enjoy the taste, especially children.

Medicinal Uses and Preparation

Native American Indians used the roots of wild licorice (or American licorice) for coughs and hoarseness. Licorice was widely used as an expectorant both here and in Europe. It is soothing to the throat and other internal organs, including the bladder and kidneys. Peptic ulcers seem to respond to the plant, as does Addison's disease. For conditions that require an anti-inflammatory agent, licorice has been used with good effect. It has also proved helpful for slow, excessive, or painful menstruation.

Food

The roots are edible when boiled, and the tea is tasty and sweet.

Current Interest

Licorice is used mainly for coughs, sore throat, and could possibly prove to be effective in treating cancer (Michael A. Weiner and Janet A. Weiner, *Herbs That Heal*).

USED TO TREAT
Addison's disease
Cough
Sore throat

USED AS/FOR
Anti-inflammatory
Expectorant
Menstrual regulation

GROWING

Wild licorice can be grown by transplanting, but it grows well from the roots and rhizomes. It is invasive.

129

Caution

Do not take large amounts of licorice over a long period of time. People have reported toxic symptoms after eating very large amounts of licorice candy (between six and eight ounces), due to its cortisonelike effects.

Licorice may also reduce potassium levels in the body or raise blood pressure. People with heart problems or elevated blood pressure should avoid licorice.

LICORICE TEA FOR SORE THROATS

1/2 teaspoon dried powdered licorice
1/2 teaspoon dried mullein or horehound
1 cup cool water

Place the water and dried herbs in a pan. Bring the mixture to a boil, remove from heat, cover, and let cool.

Licorice, when combined with other herbs, will enhance their effectiveness (Michael Moore, *Medicinal Plants of the Desert and Canyon West*).

Magnolia

Magnolia

A dinosaur? Well, maybe magnolias aren't exactly dinosaurs, but their family was probably one of the "bushes" those big animals played around. According to fossil findings, magnolias have been here for 10 to 60 million years.

Magnolias have an elegance that emits the perfume of the Old South. Louisiana claims it as its state flower, and Mississippi claims it as its state tree. Magnolias of one species or another grow along the eastern coast into Florida and across the Gulf states into Texas.

Medicinal Uses and Preparation

Most magnolia species are used in medicine. The bark is harvested in the spring or summer, and sometimes the cones are most often made into preparations. The bark can be dried and powdered and then made into a decoction or tea, or it can be tinctured while the bark is fresh in the spring or summer. Some Native American Indian tribes used the leaves as tea.

The bark of the tree, and sometimes the leaves, have been used as a muscle relaxant that aids in stomach problems such as spasms, severe diarrhea, cramps, vomiting, coughs, and even asthma. It is also an astringent and used

USED TO TREAT
Asthma
Consumption
Cough
Cramps
Diarrhea
Malaria
Nervous stomach
Parasite
Rheumatism
Sores
Toothache
Wounds

USED AS/FOR
Antiemetic
Astringent
Douche
Muscle relaxant
Quinine substitute
Tonic

GROWING

Most magnolia trees are grown on the East Coast and along the Gulf of Mexico and may be bought in most nurseries in those regions.

for toothache and on sores, wounds, and ulcers. Serious diseases such as malaria and consumption have been treated with magnolia. It is often used interchangeably with quinine. Severe rheumatism is also said to respond to the tincture. It is aromatic and given as a tonic. The cones were once dried, powdered, and made into a decoction for the treatment of worms and for use as a cleansing douche.

Food

Children in the Gulf Coast states eat the seeds as nuts.

Current Interest

Magnolia has been used as a substitute for quinine with no harmful side effects. There have been claims that addiction to tobacco can be cured with tea made of magnolia bark.

BARK DECOCTION OF MAGNOLIA

2 rounded teaspoons shaved magnolia bark
1 pint distilled water

In an enamel or glass pan, combine the water (cold) and add the bark. Bring to a boil and simmer for 20 to 30 minutes. Measure the liquid and add enough cold water to make 16 ounces. Strain. This decoction will keep up to 3 days in the refrigerator. Take 1 tablespoon as needed, up to 1 cup per day. For external use, double the amount of the bark.

Algerita with flower

Algerita with fruit

Aloe

Amaranth, red

Apache-plume

Amaranth, green

Bee balm,
spotted

Purple
horsemint

Oswego tea

Blackberries in bloom

Blackberries

Bloodweed

Buttonbush

Brier

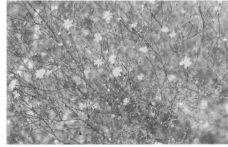

Broomweed

Castor bean

Catalpa

Catnip

Catclaw

Century plant

Cattail

Chaparral

Chaste tree

Chickweed

Cinquefoil

Cleavers

Clover, sweet

Clover, crimson

Cocklebur (photo by Judith Grace)

Coneflower

Copper Canyon marigold

Corn

Cota

Dandelion

Desert willow

Devil's claw

Dock with seeds

Dock

Dodder

Evening primrose

Flax

Fleabane

Garlic

Wild onion

Crow poison

Gay-feather

Goat's head

Goat's head (flower close-up)

Goldenrod

Grape

Holly

Honeysuckle

Hop tree

Horehound (flower close-up)

Horehound

Horsetail

Indigo

Jujube

Jimsonweed with bloom

Jimsonweed with pod

Juniper

Lamb's-quarters

Larkspur, prairie

Lemon balm

Lemongrass

Licorice, wild

Magnolia

Maidenhair fern

Mallow

Mesquite in bloom

Mesquite with beans

Milkweed with open pod

Antelope-horns in bloom

Milkweed in bloom

Mint, wild

Mullein

Mustard

Buffalo burs

Nightshade, silver-leaved

Oats

Old-man's-beard

Passionflower

Periwinkle

Poke with blooms and berries

Plantain

Poke greens

Prairie tea

Prickly pear in bloom

Prickly pear with fruit

Prickly poppy

Purslane

Queen's delight

Ratney

Redbud

Rose, Cherokee

Sagebrush

Sage, mealy

Saw palmetto

Self-heal

Senna

Shepherd's purse

Skullcap   (photo by Reed Lewis)

Soapberry

Soapwort

Spiderwort

Stonecrop

Sumac

Sumac, three-leaved

Sunflower

Jerusalem artichoke

Teasel

Trumpet vine

Vervain

Violet

Watercress

Spatterdock

Yellow lotus seedpod

Willow

Yarrow

Yucca

Yucca seedpod

Maidenhair Fern   *Adiantum*

The spring bubbled from a small cave in the Arbuckle Mountains and flowed toward the pond. I stood very still. Maybe I'd see the Little People. I didn't, but I saw their miniature fans. They were a bright green and clung to thin black stems standing near the source of the water. The background was a waterfall that filled the pond. This ran into a wide creek teeming with trout and shaded by trees—a perfect setting for maidenhair fern, a lover of water.

Medicinal Uses and Preparation

Leaves of maidenhair fern may be dried either in loose bunches or spread out on paper. Because maidenhair fern is not a plant with strong medicine, increase the amount of the herb to make tea—use one or more tablespoons in one cup of hot water.

The tea is used for the treatment of coughs, fever, chills, bronchitis (especially when treatment is begun early in the disease), and congestion of the nose and chest. The tea is a stimulant for late menstruation but does not cause cramping (Michael Moore, *Medicinal Plants of the Mountain West*).

Other uses are for stings or bites, and for getting rid of worms. Some Native tribes used the powdered leaves as a

USED TO TREAT
Asthma
Bites and stings
Bronchitis
Chills
Congestion
Cough
Dandruff
Fever
Heart trouble
Impetigo

USED AS/FOR
Hair growth
Menstrual regulation

GROWING
Maidenhair fern grows where there is plenty of water, especially near waterfalls or springs. If proper environmental conditions can be duplicated, the plant can be cultivated.

snuff for asthma. Other tribes burned the powdered dry leaves and inhaled the smoke for heart problems; ashes were also given in water for the heart.

The tea can be used as a hair rinse for dandruff, and, by reputation, for hair growth.

Other Uses

The fronds are dried and used for flower arrangements.

Current Interest

There have been studies on animals that suggest the use of maidenhair fern for asthma may be valid.

MYTHS OF THE LITTLE PEOPLE OF THE CHEROKEES

The Little People, or the Nûñně'hĭ, or "the people who live anywhere," are immortal spirit people who live in villages under mounds in the mountains of the Cherokee people. They like music and dancing and are usually the size of children but can change themselves to look just like any Native. Another race of spirits, called the Yûñwĭ Tsunsdi', "Little People," live in caves in the mountains. They are very friendly but don't like to be disturbed at home. There are several more tribes of these spirit people and most are considered friendly though mischievous. The one unfriendly spirit is a night-roaming fire carrier, and people are afraid of this one.

There is also a group of Little People who fit the description of angels, both good and bad.

MAIDENHAIR FERN SYRUP

½ cup maidenhair fern, chopped
1 teaspoon *Echinacea* root or cone
½ cup hot water
1 cup sugar (honey may be used)

Bring the water and herbs to a boil, cover, and let the mixture steep 10 minutes. Strain, and return the liquid to the pan. Add the sugar, place over heat, and stir until the sugar is dissolved. Honey may be used instead of sugar; if this is done, add it to the strained tea and heat to boiling while stirring, then remove from the heat. Place the syrup in a clean bottle or jar; a little mint or ginger can be added for taste. Take 1 teaspoon as needed for cough and congestion.

Mallow

Malva

USED TO TREAT

Arthritis

Bronchitis

Burns

Congestion

Cough

Emphysema

Gastritis

Heartburn

Indigestion

Mouth ulcers

Sore throat

Wounds

USED AS/FOR

Anti-inflammatory

Astringent

Diuretic

Food

The high mallow, *Malva sylvestris*, also known as the common mallow, may be found in many gardens. It grows well and matures quickly. There are many mallows throughout the United States, such as marsh mallow (*Althaea officinalis*) and hollyhock (*Althea rosea*). Some are common to moist areas or shady woods, others can be found in mountainous regions. The hollyhock—the staple of Old World gardens—grows in gardens and it is effective medicinally even in the cities.

Medicinal Uses and Preparation

My garden is filled with high mallow, and it is one of my personal "weeds." When my doctor told me it was dangerous to continue taking Tagamet over an extended period, I went in search of help from nature.

A high mallow plant had come up in my garden and I knew nothing about its qualities, but it was pretty. I began to research the plant and found it was a medicinal treasure. I made cold tea from all parts of the plant, and problems I had been having with my stomach were taken care of. The tea was great for heartburn and indigestion.

GROWING

Mallow seeds grow well. They should be planted in the fall or the following spring. Wild mallow will bloom in the spring through the fall. Hollyhock takes another season to grow.

136

I plant seeds in the fall and the spring, and in about six weeks, the mallow is ready to use. When winter comes along, I pot a few plants and bring them into the house. Mallow is very winter hardy. The leaves, flowers, and split root can be dried for winter use. Our winters are mild, however, and I can't say how mallow would survive below eighteen degrees Fahrenheit.

The mallow contains mucilage, and a cold infusion is soothing to mucous membranes and skin inflammations. A poultice of fresh or dried plant gives a boost of healing because it is an astringent (Michael Moore, *Medicinal Plants of the Desert and Canyon West*).

The plant can be dried, frozen, or used fresh. If used fresh for tea, it has a nice green taste, like the smell of fresh-cut grass. I usually put in a fresh mallow blossom if one is available. This gives the tea a touch of flower flavor. In most instances it is recommended that the tea be made by the cold infusion method. The plants may be gathered at any season for medicinal purposes.

The Cherokees made an ointment of mallow flowers for sores. Others made poultices for tumors, and some used it for arthritis and wounds (James A. Duke, *Handbook of Northeastern Indian Medicinal Plants*).

Mallow has been relied upon for treatment of bladder irritation, sore throat, irritated mouth, burns, wounds, sores, cough, to loosen congestion, as a diuretic, for emphysema, gastritis, bronchitis, and as an anti-inflammatory.

Food

Mallow leaves may be added to stew, soup, or gumbo as a thickening. After all, mallow is related to okra. The young seed pods may be pickled, and small new leaves may be cooked as greens (Lee Allen Peterson, *Edible Wild Plants*). The plant is a nutritious addition to any diet.

Marshmallows (the candy kind) originated with this plant. However, the original confection probably had little resemblance to our modern marshmallows. Early marshmallows were made by hand and used the root of the plant. Today other ingredients are used to produce the fluffy campfire food.

Current Interest

Root extracts show activity against tuberculosis (Steven Foster and James A. Duke, *Eastern/Central Medicinal Plants*).

There are no toxic ingredients in mallow, but after I worked with hollyhock leaves, my hands were stinging. This has not happened to me with other mallows, so I probably have one of those individual sensitivities that can happen to anyone.

COLD MALLOW TEA

2 to 3 tablespoons fresh herb (or 2 teaspoons dried herb)
1 pint cool water

Wash the herb and break it into pieces. If the root is used, chop it. Place the herb in a jar, pour the water over it, and cover. Let it sit for 6 to 8 hours.

Take ¼ to ½ cup three to four times daily, or more frequently if needed for stomach problems. Keep the tea in the refrigerator. I have kept tea this way for about 5 days. If it is made double strength it can be frozen in ice-cube trays for on-hand use. Place a cube in a cup and add cold water.

Mesquite

Prosopis

It is very hard to think of mesquite as a treasure trove. Actually, it is hard to think of it as anything but a scraggly little tree with thorns that provides thin shade. But after looking more closely, you may appreciate it for what it is. In fact, it has a certain grace with those lacy leaves blowing, and I'm sure the cattle appreciate the scanty shade, which is much better than none at all.

In the spring the long pale yellow spikes of flowers can be seen swaying among the leaves. Many similar-looking trees have flowers that are fluffy-looking balls.

Medicinal Uses and Preparation

A basic tea can be made from mesquite stems, leaves, or bark, and it may be taken both internally and externally. It has been used as an eyewash, for cuts or scrapes and swelling and bruising. Mesquite can also be taken as a treatment for diarrhea and other stomach upsets. The sap is gathered, dissolved in water, and gargled for a sore

USED TO TREAT
Colitis
Diarrhea
Gastritis
Sore throat
Stomachache

USED AS/FOR
Antiseptic
Astringent
Dye
Eyewash
Food

GROWING

There is a large mesquite tree or trees growing in my front yard—whether it is one or two trees has always puzzled me. Many people would disagree with me that having a mesquite in the yard is a good thing, but I have enjoyed it. The scanty shade helps protect plants, and the tree is a constant topic of conversation because it appears to come right from the house foundation. A storm took one side down, but it was treated and the roots were covered with potting soil. It stands up to almost anything, including heat.

139

throat; it is also soothing for stomach and intestinal problems like colitis and gastritis. Eyedrops made from the pods have been used for pinkeye (Michael Moore, *Medicinal Plants of the Desert and Canyon West*).

Food

Mesquite beans were a major food supply for Native American Indians at one time. They still are in certain areas in Mexico. One of the reasons the tree is so important is that it is plentiful even in drought conditions. The pods are high in carbohydrates and protein and contain many necessary minerals such as calcium and iron.

Mesquite can produce very sweet pods from which syrup can be made. It also makes very good jelly when the pods have reached the pink-speckled stage. Break a pod and taste it to judge the sweetness. If it is sweet, it will be good to cook with.

Other Uses

The wood can be carved, made into gunstocks, and used as fuel in barbecue grills. It has also been used as a black dye, face paint, and hair coloring.

Caution

The wind-blown pollen can cause allergies.

MESQUITE EYEWASH

3 mesquite bean pods
1 cup cold distilled water
¼ teaspoon salt

Wash the mesquite beans and bruise them by pounding. Break them into pieces. Add them to the water and salt. Bring to a boil, then turn off the heat. Cover, and let steep for 15 minutes. Make a fresh batch for each use.

This is good for irritated eyes and to treat pinkeye in people or animals.

Milkweed   *Asclepias*

Follow the monarch butterfly and you will eventually find the bright orange flowers of the butterfly weed. The monarch lays its eggs among the leaves, where they hatch. This nursery offers food and protection for the caterpillar and the new butterfly.

There are many milkweeds, but only a few are discussed here. The butterfly weed is A. *tuberosa*, commonly called chigger weed, flux weed, pleurisy root, and witch weed.

Medicinal Uses and Preparation

Butterfly weed is the easiest milkweed to identify because the flower is orange (not two-toned). The common milkweed, A. *speciosa*, is found in the West and has a pink ball of flowers on a straight stem about two feet tall. The leaves are oval and wide and grow opposite each other. The antelope-horns, A. *asperula*, has a creamy light green flower with a purple center. Most of the milkweeds are used in much the same way medicinally, but the butterfly weed is the most frequently used. All are poisonous to some extent.

The Cherokees use butterfly weed as a laxative, but when the seeds are boiled in fresh milk, it is used for diarrhea. The weed is also used for pleurisy, stomach and intestinal problems, and for the lungs. Heart problems were

USED TO TREAT
Asthma
Bronchitis
Diarrhea
Fever
Heart trouble
Intestinal problems
Pleurisy
Pneumonia
Rheumatism
Snakebite
Stomach problems
Warts

USED AS/FOR
Anti-inflammatory
Antiseptic
Diaphoretic
Diuretic
Emetic
Expectorant

GROWING

Butterfly weed is used extensively in gardens. The beautiful clumps of orange flowers will guarantee the visits of butterflies.

141

often treated with root tea (Paul B. Hamel and Mary U. Chiltoskey, *Cherokee Plants—Their Uses: A 400-Year-Old History*). Other Native American Indian uses included treatment for swellings, fever, and pneumonia.

Native American Indians and settlers used milkweed frequently as a diuretic, to cause sweating, as an expectorant, as an emetic, for rheumatism, and for snakebite. The root has been powdered and mixed with water for use on skin. The tea is used for asthma, bronchitis, swelling, and as a bronchial dilator. Use a scant teaspoon of the root, a bit less than usual, to make a boiled tea. Butterfly weed has no milky sap, but other milkweeds do. The sap of all milkweeds is well known for taking off warts.

Other Uses

Milkweed has been used in Native ceremonials in which the participants drink it for a cleansing accomplished by vomiting.

Current Interest

It has been proven that there is "estrogenic activity" in butterfly weed, and therefore, it has been given for some uterine problems (Lesley Bremness, *Herbs*).

Caution

All milkweeds are poisonous if taken in large doses. The more narrow-leaved the plant, the more toxic it is. I do not recommend using the plant internally because there are plenty of other common non-toxic plants that will substitute satisfactorily.

SECOND-HAND PROTECTION

The butterfly weed is the chosen plant on which monarch butterflies lay their eggs. The eggs are laid in the plant, and the caterpillars eat their birthplace. As butterflies, they carry the milkweed poison in their systems. If an uninstructed bird should eat a monarch butterfly, it will become sick. It is an instructed bird from then on.

The viceroy butterfly, which looks like the monarch, uses this natural protection to its advantage. Birds, thinking the viceroy is just another monarch, leave it alone.

Mint   *Mentha*

Mint is recognized in all parts of the world. Children know the odor of spearmint and are quick to smile at the red stripes of peppermint candy canes. Many mints are native to the United States and can be found near springs, creeks, and lakes. One of the main characteristics of all mints is the square stem.

Medicinal Uses and Preparation

Mint can be used fresh or dried in bundles and stored in airtight containers for later use. Spearmint and peppermint have been used especially for problems with digestion or gas. It has long been a remedy for colic in babies. Adults may get relief by chewing fresh mint or drinking tea made from the fresh or dried plant. The tea has been used for pneumonia, menstrual cramps, headaches, fever, croup, and for viral infections. It has also been a standby for colds, complaints of nervousness, and sore throats. A decoction can be made by boiling the leaves and using the tea as a wash to get rid of the itch of scabies. Besides many of the above treatments, Native American Indians used mints for cleansing in the sweat lodge. Some tribes used mint as an inhalant for nausea, headaches, and to improve concentration.

Pennyroyal has a rather unpleasant odor and has been used as an insect repellent. It is also used to relieve coughs

USED TO TREAT
Colic
Cough
Croup
Digestion
Fever
Gas
Headache
Nausea
Menstrual pain
Nerves
Pneumonia
Rheumatism
Scabies
Sore muscles
Sore throat
Virus
USED AS/FOR
Diaphoretic
Food seasoning
Insect repellent
Tea

GROWING

Mint is easily grown from plants, roots, or seed. It likes plenty of water and does well with a water source nearby. Most nurseries have mints.

143

and promote sweating. It is used on the skin for the painful joints of rheumatism.

Food

Mints make excellent drinks, both cold and hot. They are used as flavoring for candies, cakes, and many other foods. The leaves may be dried and saved to make tea. The dried leaves are frequently mixed with other herbs for different teas.

Other Uses

In the Middle Ages, mint was strewn on floors to get rid of unwanted odors. Many modern personal products contain mint, including cosmetics, deodorant, toothpaste, and mouthwash.

Current Interest

Today, one of the main uses of mint is to aid digestion and alleviate gas pains.

Caution

Pennyroyal should not be used during pregnancy because it could cause abortion. It can also cause convulsions leading to coma if taken in large doses. Severe liver damage is also possible (Reader's Digest, *Magic and Medicine of Plants*).

MINT OIL RUB

Using either peppermint or pennyroyal, fill a jar loosely with the fresh herb. Cover the mint with vegetable or mineral oil and cap. Place the jar in a dark place and shake several times a day for ten days. Strain, and place the oil in a dark bottle or keep in a cool dark place.

This may be rubbed on sore muscles or joints to relieve pain.

Mullein   *Verbascum Thapsus*

At night a procession might have been seen winding down mountain paths or along a slope. Those living in the area knew what was happening, for they'd grown up with it. This was a group of worshippers who carried the mullein plant, stripped of leaves and dipped in wax, to light their way in a processional or ceremonial. This scene could have been common in many places and many eras, because diverse cultures and religions have used such lights in this way.

Even today, in many places mullein carries the idea of evil—or good, according to belief. In spite of the fact that mullein claims the attention of anyone who looks, it is a neglected plant. It has large leaves, up to seven inches by fourteen inches, which are thick and furry and laid out in an attractive rosette. The tall stem topped with butter-colored flowers is thought of by many as a weed.

Medicinal Uses and Preparation

The leaves and flowers of mullein are most commonly used, and occasionally the root is. A basic tea can be made from

USED TO TREAT
Bronchitis
Burns
Congestion
Cough
Earache
Migraine
Sore throat
USED AS/FOR
Anti-inflammatory
Antiseptic
Antispasmodic
Expectorant
Sedative

GROWING

Those who have opened their gardens to mullein—whether it is called flannel-leaf, Jacob's staff, old man's flannel, candlewick, Aaron's rod, or velvet plant—are not sorry. It is a beautiful background or frame for the garden and may be transplanted. The plants are easily grown from seed, which form after the flowers have fallen, and the rod becomes like a giant pepper shaker full of seed. The seed can also be bought from native-plant nurseries and catalogs.

145

the leaves, flowers, or both. Mullein contains an anti-inflammatory and is antispasmodic and expectorant. This is a tea I use for my family when they have coughs, sore throats, or bronchitis. It is soothing and has a sedative quality.

The leaves have been used to make tea to treat wounds and sores because of their healing qualities, and they have been applied directly to the skin as bandages. Tincture can be made from the leaves and has been used by some Native American Indian tribes for migraine headaches and earaches. Flower tea is taken for sedation or pain.

Poultices can be made of leaves and applied to sore areas. This is done by adding hot water or vinegar to whole leaves and letting them sit until they are cool enough to avoid burning.

A flower infusion in oil can be made and used for skin problems or placed warm in the ear for earaches. Unhealed wounds or ulcers can also benefit from this oil.

Other Uses

The plants have been used to ward off witches, and have also been described as being used by witches. One way to prevent pregnancy, so I've been told, is to put a mullein leaf in the shoe. On the other hand (or foot), one might ensure pregnancy the same way. What is known for sure is that it was once a common practice to line the shoes with the wool-like leaves to keep the feet warm.

Current Interest

Scientific tests have proven that mullein contains substances that work against tuberculosis.

Caution

The leaves of mullein contain anticoagulant, and rotenone, an insecticide, and should not be used during pregnancy, nor should anyone taking an anticoagulant use mullein. The flowers, however, are on the Generally Recognized as Safe (GRAS) list sponsored by the U.S. Food and Drug Administration.

TO PREPARE MULLEIN TEA

1 ounce by measure fresh broken mullein leaves
2 cups hot water

Pour the water over the leaves. Cover, and steep for 10 to 15 minutes. Strain through several layers of cloth or a coffee filter to remove the tiny hairs. Sip on the tea as needed for a dry, hacking cough. Honey may be added to make it more palatable. If congestion occurs, I add 1 teaspoon of horehound leaf.

Mustard *Brassica*

Throughout the four seasons, wild mustard can be seen along roadsides, in fields, and along the edges of woods. In the winter it has many leaves, and through most of the year it has small yellow flowers. In late summer and fall, seedpods appear. This is the part that is used in medicine.

Medicinal Uses and Preparation

Dried seeds can be made into plasters, ointments, and mixed with water. The seeds have been used internally, but most often are applied to the skin. Mustard seeds, if taken in large quantities, can be toxic.

Applied as a plaster, mustard stimulates circulation and is used on the chest for colds, lung congestion, bronchitis, and for sore muscles. An ointment made of the seed can be rubbed on the chest, joints, and muscles.

The seeds have been used as a laxative, for toothache, and for indigestion. However, the seeds can be irritating to the stomach and intestines, so it is best to try only a small amount at first, then to limit the amount.

Native American Indians have used the dried powdered seeds as a healing snuff for dropsy (swelling of the extremities due to poor circulation), fever, colds, and asthma.

USED TO TREAT

Asthma

Bronchitis

Congestion

Constipation

Dropsy

Fever

Indigestion

Sore muscles

Toothache

USED AS/FOR

Food

GROWING

Mustard is easily grown from seed.

Food

The young leaves can be eaten raw in salads or cooked as greens. The seeds can be prepared as mustard spread.

Current Interest

One teaspoon of powdered mustard seeds mixed in one cup of water can be given for poisoning. This is an emetic and will cause vomiting. Make sure the poison that has been taken is not caustic (a substance that will damage tissues, such as acid) before giving the mustard water, or it will burn the mouth and throat when vomited. Always call for professional help in case of poisoning.

Caution

Care should be taken when using mustard plasters. They can blister the skin if left too long.

Mustard can be toxic if taken in large amounts.

HOW TO MAKE A MUSTARD PLASTER

1 level tablespoon mustard powder (powdered dried seeds)
2 cups flour or cornmeal

Stir the two dry ingredients together and pour lukewarm water over them until it makes a paste. Use a large piece of cotton cloth and spread the paste on one side to the size needed to cover the area to be treated. Coat the skin with oil or grease before applying the plaster. Double the cloth over sandwich-fashion, and apply it wherever it is needed. Cover it with a towel. The treated area will become very warm and must be watched carefully to prevent overexposure and burning. Leave the plaster on for no more than 20 minutes.

This is a recipe that was used by early settlers and my grandmother and mother. It was mostly used for congestion of the lungs or bad colds.

Mustard

MUSTARD SPREAD
(NOT FOR THE FAINT-HEARTED)

⅓ cup ground mustard seed
⅓ cup wheat flour
Mix ⅓ cup vinegar and ⅓ cup water
Add 1 teaspoon salt
And 1 teaspoon honey

Brown the flour in a skillet and then pour the flour into a bowl. Mix in the mustard seed and salt. Add the vinegar, water, and honey, and stir until the mixture becomes a smooth paste. Store in the refrigerator.

Nightshade

Solanum

Nightshade conjures up words like death, poison, and black magic. Included in our thoughts along this line may be such plants as deadly nightshade, horse nettle, and buffalo bur, but we probably don't think of potatoes, tomatoes, and eggplant, cousins of nightshade.

Medicinal Uses and Preparation

Nightshade has been used in Europe and here in the United States by Indians and settlers alike. Today it is little used except externally, because it is not safe.

Several Indian tribes used the plant internally to treat tuberculosis, to get rid of worms, or just as a blood cleanser. Nightshade was also considered an antispasmodic. It was given for fevers, eye problems, sleeplessness, and even rabies (James A. Duke, *Handbook of Northeastern Indian Medicinal Plants*).

Nightshade salves were made and used for skin problems and sores by Indians and settlers alike.

The *Dispensatory of the United States 1836* suggests the use of the leaves internally and also externally to treat cancer and other painful diseases, including skin ulcers.

USED TO TREAT
Eye irritation
Fever
Insomnia
Parasite
Rabies
Skin problems
Tuberculosis

USED AS/FOR
Antispasmodic
Blood purification
Food

GROWING

There are two wild nightshades that are very pretty. One is the silver-leaved nightshade. It has deep blue flowers with bright yellow stamens. The other is the buffalo bur, which has bright yellow flowers. These are very plentiful in the wild and therefore have two drawbacks: They are covered with stickers and they are toxic. Children in the garden may find the bright yellow fruit about the size of a marble tempting—and highly poisonous.

151

Food

People have used nightshade for food in many parts of the world. Some species, when handled properly, can be eaten. Also, the part of the plant to be eaten must be considered. The berries of the black nightshade, when ripe, have been cooked in pies and safely eaten. The poison in some berries decreases as they get black and ripen; however, after finding this out, I bit into a ripened black berry of the nightshade. I am convinced it was definitely poison. Some of the poison may be decreased by cooking, but I wouldn't recommend it.

Current Interest

It has been found that nightshade inhibits the growth of cancer cells.

Caution

Nightshade has the potential to be extremely poisonous. Do not use internally.

THE GOOD AND BAD OF POTATOES

Potatoes, a member of the nightshade family, are not only a basic food that contains many vitamins and minerals, but they can also turn deadly. The potato plant is poisonous, as are green potatoes or those with green color, which can develop when they are left in the sun. The same applies to sprouted potatoes. People and animals have died from eating green or sprouted potatoes. Other food plants within the nightshade family are tomato, eggplant, and tomatillo. Every part of these plants is poisonous except the fruit.

Oat

Avena

The oat is a food we connect to childhood and that follows us into old age. Oats have always been known as a healthful food, and we now know much more about this. Oats are not only good to eat, but the whole plant makes good medicine.

Medicinal Uses and Preparation

Oat can be used green or dry, and the grain, stem, or leaves may be used. Oat tea or tincture has been used for anxiety and depression. Oat tea makes a good wash for skin problems, and sitz baths of oatmeal may help bladder and genital problems. An oat footbath might help with tired achy feet or rough scaly skin.

Native American Indians used oat for diarrhea and as a blood purifier; the tea or tincture can be used for these purposes. The plant was made into a poultice for fractures and boils. Poultices of oatmeal have also been used for some skin diseases, cold sores, and eczema.

Food

The main use for oats has always been food. Oats are easily digested and also provide fiber in the diet. Besides this, they contain vitamin B, phosphorus, iron, aluminum,

USED TO TREAT
Boils
Cold sores
Depression
Diarrhea
Eczema
Fractures
Nerves
Skin problems
Sore throat

USED AS/FOR
Blood purification
Food
Sedative
Vitamins

GROWING

Oat may be grown from seed or may be gathered in the wild. There is a North American native oat, but the cultivated variety has escaped and is plentiful in the wild.

potassium, manganese, cobalt, and vitamins A, D, and E (Mannfried Phklow, *Healing Plants*).

Current Interest

Oat has been found to lower cholesterol and reduce the incidence of colon cancer (Michael A. Weiner and Janet A. Weiner, *Herbs That Heal*).

TINCTURE OF OATS

Chop green oats and put them into a canning jar. Fill the jar, but do not pack it tightly. Pour in Everclear (or vodka) until it just covers the herb. Seal.

Keep the jar in a dark place for fourteen days. Shake the jar frequently. Strain the mixture, and store the liquid tincture in an amber container, or keep it in the dark.

Use five drops of tincture of oats several times a day for nervousness. Use twenty to twenty-five drops one hour before bedtime for sedation (Mannfried Phklow, *Healing Plants*).

Old-Man's-Beard   *Clematis*

Old-man's-beard, sometimes called virgin's bower, does not sound appealing, but though the name does somewhat describe this unusual plant, old-man's-beard has its own charm. This long winding vine crawls on fences and weaves among plants, forming big mats with toothed leaves and creamy-colored flowers that are so quiet they are hardly noticed. But as with most plain blooms, a close look tells another story. The blossoms have real character and their own beauty. They don't rival the fruit, though. This shows up as a tightly packed bundle of very narrow feathers that wave out beyond the seed several inches. In the fall, the fluffs attached to the seed are attention-getters. The whole plant is a mass of waving plumes and is hard to miss.

> **USED TO TREAT**
> Headache
> Nerves
> Stomachache

Medicinal Uses and Preparation

This plant is controversial. Although some declare it dangerous, others have found it useful. It has been used by the Native American Indians as a tea made from the roots for the nerves and stomach problems, and across the world in China it is a remedy in Chinese medicine as a painkiller for a number of ailments. The leaves are used in ointments and for pain relief.

GROWING

If you have a large space near a fence, you may have just the spot for old-man's-beard.

Gather the vines and dry them before working with them—they can irritate the hands. After drying, they can be cut into very small pieces for storage.

Caution

Old-man's-beard is reported by some sources to be toxic. The vines can cause a rash if handled.

TEA FOR MIGRAINES

1 teaspoon dried, chopped old-man's-beard leaf and vine
1 cup hot water

Put the herb in a cup and pour hot water over it. Cover, and steep 15 to 20 minutes, then strain.

Start taking the tea as soon as you feel a headache coming on.

Passionflower   *Passiflora*

There are over 350 species of passionflower native to the United States, and the rest of the world has 40 more. This is one of the most beautiful flowers in the country. Even the fruit and vine offer a fitting frame for display of the bloom, but it has never been dependent on looks alone for its popularity. Native American Indians used the plant since long before the settlers arrived, and this is a case of the same plant being used similarly on different continents.

Other names for passionflower are maypop, passionaria (from the Spanish), and passion-fruit vine. The flowers are lavender or cream and are found in all parts of the East, South, West, and Southwest.

Medicinal Uses and Preparation

Gather leaves, stems, and flowers. These may be used fresh or dried. The plant can be made into a tea or a tincture. Dosage is four to eight ounces of tea made of one-half to one teaspoon dry herb, or one-half teaspoon of tincture can be taken every four hours, three times a day. The plant is sometimes used as a poultice: Roots of two plants are most potent but not safe during pregnancy. One of the passionflower's main uses is for sedation. It is calming but not depressive. It relieves anxiety and relaxes muscles.

USED TO TREAT
Boils
Cramps
Diarrhea
Epilepsy
Insomnia
Morning sickness
Neuralgia
Wounds

USED AS/FOR
Antiseptic
Antispasmodic
Food
Muscle relaxant
Sedative

GROWING

This is a very popular plant, and although it grows wild, it may be scarce in certain areas. Pick the plant only if it is found in a densely populated colony. Maypops are available in many nurseries.

Passionflower is an antispasmodic and reduces or eliminates cramps of diarrhea and menstrual cramps, along with morning sickness, anxiety, neuralgia, and restlessness. Passionflower has also been used in the treatment of epilepsy.

Food

The fruit is oval and yellow in most eastern areas, and red in others. It is filled with seeds reminiscent of pomegranates. They contain some vitamin A and niacin and are used in drinks and jellies—at least those that haven't been eaten fresh. It has a mild, flowerlike taste.

Current Interest

Passionflower causes very good sedation that decreases blood pressure and slows the heartbeat. For those who are restless at night and can't sleep, passionflower might be the answer. The plant is safe, even for small children and babies.

Caution

Do not exceed the recommended dosage. Passionflower has been used on a long-term basis with no problems. The roots should not be taken during pregnancy.

PASSIONFLOWER

When the Spanish invaders came into South America, their priests looked closely at the passionflower and saw symbols of the crucifixion of Christ. There are a total of ten sepals and petals, which represented the apostles, excluding Judas and Peter. The fringe represented the crown of thorns, and the five stamens were Christ's wounds. The three stigmas were the nails used on the cross or possibly the Trinity, and the tendrils were the whips used to scourge Christ.

Periwinkle

Vinca major

The first colonists in New England brought the periwinkle and used it as a medicinal and garden flower. The evergreen foliage and bright blue flowers spread through the United States, Canada, and Mexico, and were used by later settlers and Native American Indians alike.

Medicinal Uses and Preparation

Collect all the aerial parts of the plant, including the flower. It may be dried and later used as a tea or tincture. Periwinkle stimulates circulation peripherally but also is a strong capillary constrictor. Because of these properties it is used successfully for headache, depending on the individual. The usual dose is one-half teaspoon of the tincture or one-half cup of tea, taken several times a day (Michael Moore, *Medicinal Plants of the Desert and Canyon West*).

The plant also aids in stopping nosebleed when a fresh leaf or powdered dried plant is applied topically in the nose.

The tea or tincture may be used as a sedative, to decrease menstrual flow or uterine bleeding, to stop diarrhea, and to stanch bleeding of the mouth. It also brings about some lowering of blood pressure. It is astringent and useful for stanching bleeding wounds. Periwinkle may be chewed for toothache.

USED TO TREAT

Diarrhea

Headache

Hemorrhoids

High blood pressure

Nosebleed

Sore throat

Toothache

Wounds

USED AS/FOR

Astringent

Sedative

GROWING

Periwinkle is easily grown from a cutting, seed, or from whole plants, which can be bought in most nurseries. It likes shade and water, but it can often be found growing in bright sunlight. The plant is invasive, and this should be a consideration when planting.

159

Current Interest

A related plant, Madagascar periwinkle (*Catharanthus roseus*), has been used as a treatment for a number of types of cancer, including tumors, Hodgkin's disease, and leukemia. However, healthy cells are also affected by the treatment.

Caution

The Madagascar periwinkle is poisonous.

A LOVE POTION

This is from *The boke of secretes of Albartus Magnus of the vertues of Herbes, Stones, and certaine beastes* printed by William Copland. The author was unknown. "Perwynke when it is beate unto pouder with wormes of ye earth wrapped aboute it and with an herbe called houslyke it induceth love between man and wyfe if it bee used in their meales . . . (Eleanour Sinclair Rohde, *The Old English Herbals*)

Plantain

Plantago

Waste areas are the first places to look for plantains. The plants have long oval leaves stemming from a dusty green basal rosette. From the center, one or more spikes shoot straight up with a thickening at the upper end that bears inconspicuous greenish flowers. Later, dark seeds appear, giving the plant a speckled appearance. The whole plant is easily overshadowed by any bright growth, but it is not hard to see.

Plantain has been and continues to be an important plant to many people throughout the world. In its native Eurasia it has a long history, and Native American Indians have used plantain since it was brought to North America. The plantain was carried by the early American colonists for food and medicine in the late 1600s. James A. Duke, in his book *Handbook of Edible Weeds*, says that the seeds "have been found in the stomachs of mummified 'bog people' of the 4th century northern Europe." In fact, many of the same uses for plantain are practiced in widely spaced geographic areas.

Medicinal Uses and Preparation

Use plantain fresh or dried. It has been used for poultices, as a tea, a decoction, and for ear and eyedrops.

USED TO TREAT

Bruises

Bites

Burns

Cancer

Cough

Diarrhea

Dysentery

High blood pressure

Infections

Rheumatism

Snakebite

Stomachache

Warts

USED AS/FOR

Anti-inflammatory

Antiseptic

Douche

Food

Weight loss

GROWING

It will probably not be necessary to cultivate this plant, because it will usually show up whether you want it or not. However, it will grow from seed, which can be picked from plants in most alleys or vacant lots. A few plants placed not too near one another can grow into fairly large and attractive specimens.

 161

The leaves have been used for poultices for rheumatism, inflammation, swelling, burns, wounds, infections, sores, bruises, snakebites, and bug bites. Some of the poultices seem to be the type that might be used as first-aid for insect bites, with no niceties involved—the plant is chewed, then placed on the area (Michael Moore, *Medicinal Plants of the Mountain West*).

Plantain tea has been used in much the same way, as a wash or taken by mouth for such problems as bites, infected or inflamed kidneys, or as a douche. Leaf tea has been used for dysentery, diarrhea, and to prevent or ease coughs, stomachache, and intestinal problems. A decoction can also be made. The fresh juice has been used for stomach ulcers, and the roots have been used in the treatment of cancer and warts.

The dried leaves and roots can be useful to help a child with lung problems. The dosage is one scant teaspoon with one cup of hot water made into a tea to be given each morning (Michael Moore, *Medicinal Plants of the Mountain West*).

Food

Young plants can be eaten, but identification can be a problem—there are some poisonous plants that look like young plantain.

Current Interest

It is thought that plantain seeds may lower blood pressure. The plant does kill microorganisms and increases the healing rate (Steven Foster and James A. Duke, *Eastern/Central Medicinal Plants*).

Caution

Wait until the flowering stalk is present before identifying the plant. There are plants similar to plantain that are toxic.

SEED HUSKS

The seed husks of certain species of plantain are used in commercial products for regulation of the bowels. They are mixed with liquid and absorb many times their weight in water. Some weight-loss products rely on these husks in products that give the dieter a feeling of fullness and reduce the craving for food (Lesley Bremness, *Herbs*).

Poke   *Phytolacca americana*

When I think of poke, the first thing I think of is how much fun my girlhood friend and I had using the berries in our playhouses. We gathered the ripe fruit, crushed it, and put it in bottles as "grape juice." We boiled the berries to dye doll clothes and in the process dyed ourselves and our own clothes. Of course, we never put any of it in our mouths. We knew it was poisonous and were cautious about it.

As I think of the situation now, I would probably be horrified if my grandchildren did the same thing. Any open cut can absorb the poison, and what if the pretty color of the "grape juice" tempted one of them to taste it?

All parts of the poke plant have poison in them, but under the right circumstances poke has been used for several hundred years as medicine. Settlers and Native American Indians used the plant extensively. This is probably the trick: Those who have received knowledge from generations past are most apt to understand how to use the plant safely. Others would be better off to substitute other plants that offer the same cures.

USED TO TREAT
Dysentery
Hemorrhoids
Rheumatism
Sore breasts
Sprains
USED AS/FOR
Anti-inflammatory
Food

GROWING

Poke, sometimes called poke weed, is an eye-catcher with its bright green leaves and red stems. Later, the near-black berries add to its attraction, but caution should be taken to plant it in a safe place, where it won't tempt children. It grows easily from seed and roots. These aren't readily available in nurseries, but you could possibly get some seeds through a seed exchange. Seed exchanges are regular sections in some periodicals, such as *Mother Earth News*.

163

Medicinal Uses and Preparation

Poke is used as a medicine mainly for rheumatism. Both the root and berries have been used in this manner. Along the same line, swelling and sprains are supposed to benefit from the treatment, whether tea, tincture, or poultice. Poke is not generally used internally anymore because it is poisonous. At one time, though, it was used by many Native American Indian tribes and settlers.

A poke berry poultice is supposed to cure sore breasts and sores in general. The berry tea was given for dysentery. The dried root, made into a tea, was used on hemorrhoids, and a poison oak treatment was made with poke and salt water. The root does have anti-inflammatory qualities.

The leaves have been made into ointment for the eyes and as an application for sores. A poultice could be made of the leaves, because they contain some narcotic qualities that might relieve pain in some ailments.

Food

Some sources suggest that poke should not be eaten at all because it contains poison; however, it seems sad that there are those who will never have the experience of eating this very good green. It can be done safely if a few rules are followed. First, be sure you recognize the plant; it's best to have someone who knows it with you the first few times you collect it. Pick only those young plants that are not over nine inches tall and have no signs of blooms or heads on them. Wash the plant carefully, and pick off any bugs. Put it in a granite-ware, stainless steel, or glass pan. Cover with water and boil for about five minutes. Pour this water off and rinse the greens (some prefer to do this procedure twice). Add water, a little bacon, and bring the greens again to a boil. Simmer for twenty to thirty minutes. Add salt to taste and maybe some pepper sauce. Enjoy.

Current Interest

Researchers at Southwest Texas State University have done a study on a protein in poke that may prove to be antiviral and an effective treatment for flu and herpes. There are also studies of poke in the treatment of leukemia.

Caution

Poke is a poisonous plant and can be dangerous as medication. Do not use it except with the instructions of someone who is an expert in its use.

POKE SALET?

When a reference is made to "poke salet," it is not salad as we think of it. Do not eat poke raw. Poke is a potherb. The young plants should always be parboiled, rinsed once or twice, and then cooked until done.

Prairie Tea   *Croton monanthogynus*

When Mary knocked on my door and handed me several bushy plants, I smiled. This was the tea she had told me of, a plant that grew wild and that her people, African Americans in the area, had used many years ago. When I questioned her about it, she promised to ask around, but she was sure it had "died out." Now she was handing me several of the plants, and I was excited. It had reddish brown stems with numerous stiff branches, and the leaves were mostly gray-green. They were small, about one-half inch by one-quarter inch in length, without hairs. Looking closer, I found a tiny greenish flower and a few of the fruit, which were about the shape of a one-sixteenth-inch strawberry with four flat sides.

It had a nice smell, and Mary told me it should be dried before using. Later, after it was dry, I brewed a pot of tea and found it to be pale yellow in color with a pleasant taste. It is called prairie tea and can be used fresh, but it is stronger if dried. Looking around, I found the plant growing on every side road I went down. I picked several to take to Reed Lewis, an expert on native plants, and he identified it as

GROWING

This is a weedy-looking plant, and should you be looking for theme-garden plants, this would fit right into a tea garden or a garden of sweet-smelling herbs. It is easily grown from seed.

Croton monanthogynus. A number of my friends have since been introduced to it, and we all gathered enough for winter.

Medicinal Uses and Preparation

Prairie tea is one of those comfort teas you prepare and thrust into the hand of a distraught friend who has lost her job or just needs a little TLC. It calms and relaxes. Gather the whole plant and dry it. When it is completely dry, remove the leaves and store in an airtight container.

Food

Prairie tea can also be used as a spice, for instance, a substitute for basil.

Caution

There are several other species of *Croton* that may be toxic. As with any plant, certain people may be allergic to it, and it may cause skin irritation. Be certain in its identification (Delena Tull, *A Practical Guide to Edible and Useful Plants*).

A TEA FOR CALMING

½ teaspoon prairie tea
½ teaspoon passionflower vine
hot water

Put the dried herbs in a tea ball and place in a cup. Fill the cup with hot water and steep for 10 minutes. This is a good, relaxing tea when you are tired. It can also be served iced for hot weather. Sweeten with honey, if desired. To use the herbs fresh, increase their measurements to ½ tablespoon each.

Prickly Pear *Opuntia*

The Aztec Indians held the prickly pear in high esteem. Even today, their descendants, the people of Mexico, have on their flag a prickly pear cactus as the perch of an eagle and a snake. Indians of the U.S. Southwest used and still use the fruit and pads of the cactus as food and medicine. This plant is found in most every part of the United States and Mexico.

USED TO TREAT

Bites

Bruises

Burns

Diabetes

Insect bites

Rheumatism

Urinary tract infections

Warts

USED AS/FOR

Anti-inflammatory

Antiseptic

Diuretic

Food

Medicinal Uses and Preparation

Most often prickly pears are used fresh for medicine. The flowers can be dried for later use. The pads are seared over a flame to remove the stickers, skinned, and sliced for direct use, or they are mashed, put in a cloth, and squeezed to obtain the juice. The inside of the pad is sticky and jellylike, much like *Aloe vera*.

The flowers can be made into a tea to help relieve fragile capillaries.

Inflamed areas are treated with the plant, whether the kidneys and bladder, burned skin (such as sunburn or scalds), or insect bites. A peeled pad, or *nopalito,* can be sliced thin or mashed and placed on an area for treatment. Old ulcers and arthritis have supposedly responded

GROWING

Prickly pear pads are commonly planted in gardens, especially rock gardens. The plant comes with stickers or without, and the flowers range from yellow, orange, red, and bright pink to purple. One of the simplest ways to grow prickly pear is to lay a pad on the ground or in a pot where it has good contact with the dirt. It will grow without any care. It takes little water, lots of sun, and poor soil. A piece of the root will also grow, as will seeds.

well when a heated *nopalito* is applied. The pad is also a good poultice for wounds, bruises, and boils. Not only does it soothe and heal but it has a drawing quality that relieves swelling and pain.

Prickly pear can also be taken by mouth in the crushed form or as juice. This has frequently been done for urinary tract infections or any other inflammation or irritation of the mucous membranes. Prickly pear juice is also a diuretic. Tea made from the pad has been used to relieve lung problems and also used on warts. Slightly roasted and split fruit has also been used on warts.

Food

The fruit (*tunas*), whether yellow, orange, or red, can be eaten raw, dried, or candied, and can be made into jelly or syrup. The seeds or the dried fruit can be ground into a flour that can be used for thickening. The leaves or young pads are sliced and cooked with eggs or as a vegetable. Be sure to hold the fruit or pads over an open flame to burn off the stickers.

Other Uses

Cochineal scale insects make webs in which to lay eggs on the prickly pear cactus. These insects make a very good red dye.

Current Interest

The juice from the pads is taken to reduce blood sugar in adult-onset diabetes. It has also been used to lower blood cholesterol.

Caution

The stickers can be dangerous. They are painful if they prick the skin, and should they be eaten, they can lodge in the mouth and throat.

CACTUS FRUIT JELLY

3 cups prickly pear juice
4-1/2 cups sugar
1/3 cup lemon juice
1 package pectin powder

To prepare the fruit for jelly, wash off 1/2 gallon of fruit (stickers and all) and put into a stainless or enamel roast pan. Using a knife and fork, cut the fruit into pieces. Add water until the pieces are almost covered. Put on the heat and bring to a boil. Cook for 5 to 10 minutes. Use a colander lined with cloth to strain the juice. Throw away the cloth and sediment. Strain the juice again through a coffee filter or two more times through a cloth. Several layers of paper towels work well as a strainer.

Measure the juice to get 3 cups. Add water if necessary. Add the lemon juice and pectin powder. Heat, and when the mixture reaches a rolling boil, add 4-1/2 cups of sugar. Stir continuously and boil for 75 seconds. Pour immediately into sterile jars and seal.

Prickly Poppy   *Argemone polyanthemos*

The gauzy flutter of snowlike mountain rose petals reached across thirty acres. It could have been a mass of white butterflies with yellow bodies held earthbound by prickly stems—they were so alive. The sight brought to mind the Wizard of Oz or the fields of Flanders, but these were pure and white. Many call them simply poppies or white prickly poppies, but I like the name mountain rose because that's what my grandmother called them.

Medicinal Uses and Preparation

One of the main medicinal extracts from the prickly poppy is its yellow sap. It is caustic and therefore makes a good solution for warts. In a dilute form the juice can be used for heat rash, hives, and jock-itch. This makes one wonder if it would also work on ringworm. At one time the sap was used to treat the itch of scabies and has been used to treat cancer.

Gather the whole plant when it's in flower, and dry it. Tea can be made from the leaves. The tea has been used for urethra and prostate infection and for burns. It relieves pain and swelling and has sedative qualities. Its analgesic and muscle-relaxing qualities help with the cramps of diarrhea and tension before menses (Michael Moore, *Medicinal Plants of the Desert and Canyon West*).

USED TO TREAT

Burns

Cancer

Constipation

Diarrhea

Heat rash

Hemorrhoids

Hives

Itching

Prostate infection

Scabies

Scrapes

Urethra infection

Warts

USED AS/FOR

Analgesic

Emetic

Food

Sedative

GROWING

The large white poppies may be grown from seed, which should be planted in the fall for the next spring's crop. Find a patch or border where the plants can grow thickly. A field of the plant in bloom is a real eye-catcher. One thing to remember is that prickly poppy is invasive.

171

Tea made from the seed has been used to bring about vomiting; it is also a strong laxative. Ointment from the seed is good for burns, hemorrhoids, and broken skin.

Food

The seed may be eaten in small amounts.

Current Interest

In my experience, the juice works well to remove warts.

Caution

The plant's spines can pierce hands severely—use gloves when handling the plant. The juice is caustic and contains toxic alkaloids, so don't allow it to contact skin unless it is part of a treatment. Internal use is not recommended.

POPPY SEED SALVE

6 tablespoons crushed prickly poppy seeds
6 tablespoons petroleum jelly or lard

Place the seeds and petroleum jelly or lard in a small stainless steel, glass, or enamel pan. Put the pan into a larger pan that has water in it (or use a double boiler). Bring the water to a boil. Stir the seed mixture until it is melted. Turn the heat to low and leave the pan on the heat for 1 to 2 hours. Strain the mixture into jars and seal.

This salve is good for minor burns, hemorrhoids, itching, ulcers, scrapes, and other painful skin conditions. Do not use it for serious burns, however.

Purslane

Portulaca

The old Cherokee medicine man was bent from many years of stooping as he went from plant to plant. He was moving slowly and had gathered a small bundle as he moved near the purslane. He looked at it but didn't stop. Three times he came to a plant, and it wasn't until the fourth plant that he paused. Slowly he walked around the plant from right to left, muttering as he went. Then he leaned down, sought out the root section, and pulled the whole plant up. He dropped a red bead inside the hole and covered it.

Red is considered a sacred color by the Cherokees. It is the color given to the east, the place of birth and new life. Possibly the reason the red bead was put into the hole in the soil was to return something to the earth because something had been removed. It is considered proper to ask plants' permission before picking them, and tobacco is sprinkled in the plant's place. The number four is a sacred number to the Cherokees, which is perhaps why the medicine man bypassed the first three plants.

He put the plant in his bundle and started home. On the way, he came to a small creek and tossed in his

USED TO TREAT

Burns

Diarrhea

Earache

High blood pressure

Parasites

Scurvy

Sores

Stomachache

Wounds

USED AS/FOR

Anti-inflammatory

Antispasmodic

Diuretic

Food

Skin cleanser

GROWING

Purslane is grown in many gardens, hanging baskets, and pots. It is drought-resistant and is easy to transplant or start from seed.

173

bundle of herbs, all the while mumbling prayers. They popped back to the surface, and he smiled. They were good herbs; they would heal.

Purslane is a succulent that is found growing wild or in gardens as a cultivated plant. Even in the heat of summer the colorful flowers offer a freshness. They are also useful as medicine and food.

Medicinal Uses and Preparation

The plant has been used fresh, or could be tinctured. The fruit or seeds may also be collected. The crushed plant has been used for diarrhea, stomachache, sores, wounds, painful urinary problems, inflammation, scurvy, burns, and as a diuretic. Purslane has been boiled and given as a worm treatment. It is thought by some to reduce blood pressure and is used as an antispasmodic. The juice is held by the Cherokees to be a treatment for earache (Paul B. Hamel and Mary U. Chiltoskey, *Cherokee Plants—Their Uses: A 400-Year-Old History*).

In other parts of the world, the seed and fruit of the purslane are used for heart problems and breathing distress.

Food

All parts of the plant may be eaten raw and cooked. Purslane is very nutritious because it contains vitamins C and A, riboflavin, calcium, phosphorous, and iron. It may be cooked in a stir-fry, added to soups, or eaten raw in salads. The seeds can be ground and added to flour to increase its food value.

Other Uses

Purslane was a basic cosmetic for many cultures. It is both cleansing and healing, and tightens the skin. It was used for these purposes in Greece and England. It was also grown in the Arctic but was used mostly for food there.

Current Interest

Many of the uses and actions of purslane are similar to that of *Aloe vera*. It has a potential to work against cancer.

Caution

Purslane contains oxalic acid, like spinach. As with any green of this nature, purslane should not be eaten every day because the oxalic acid could prevent the absorption of calcium.

SKIN CLEANSER AND FRESHENER

1 cup chopped purslane
1 cup cool water

Place the purslane on a double layer of cheesecloth. Wrap the cloth loosely and tie it with string or a rubber band to make a bag. Place it in a bowl and mash it with a potato masher, then squeeze it by hand. Add the 1 cup of cool water to the bowl. Dip and press the bag in the water several times to wash out the juice. Squeeze the bag tightly. Store the juice in a canning jar in the refrigerator. This will keep about 5 days.

Wash the face, then apply the purslane juice to the skin. Take a rest for 3 to 5 minutes, allowing the juice to work, then rinse. Not only will this refresh the skin, but it will also smooth a few wrinkles while doing so. This is also good for acne.

Queen's Delight   *Stillingia*

Queen's delight is found on the plains and in the pine barrens of the South across Texas to eastern New Mexico. The plant is indigenous to the United States. It is a bright green plant with narrow lance-shaped leaves along the stem, which ends in a flower stalk. The female flowers are at the lower part and are small and pod-shaped, whereas the small male flowers on the upper end are yellow and have no petals.

USED TO TREAT

Athlete's foot

Constipation

Cough

Ringworm

Syphilis

Yeast infection

USED AS/FOR

Blood purification

Emetic

Medicinal Uses and Preparation

The roots are the part used for medicinal purposes. They should be dug, cleaned, and cut like carrot sticks to dry. After drying, they should be crushed into powder before making a decoction or tincture.

Queen's delight has a long history that began with the Native American Indians. It was used as a treatment for syphilis, to cleanse the blood, as a laxative, and as an emetic. It was given to new mothers as a drink and bath. The bath was also supposed to regulate menses.

The tincture can be taken for dry hacking coughs, and it is used topically on skin problems, including fungus and yeast infections that have become unresponsive to other treatments.

GROWING

Queen's delight can be transplanted or grown from seed. It's probably not available at native-plant nurseries, but check it out anyway. The bright green plant with yellow on the spike is attractive.

Current Interest

This plant enjoyed popularity up to the early twentieth century but is used infrequently now.

Caution

Fresh plants can cause problems with the stomach and intestines, causing such symptoms as diarrhea and vomiting. Overuse can also cause the same symptoms.

TINCTURE OF QUEEN'S DELIGHT

4.5 ounces (125 grams) dried queen's delight root, crushed finely
350 milliliters grain alcohol (such as Everclear)
250 milliliters distilled water

Use part of the liquid to wet down the crushed herb, then add the rest of the liquid. Keep the mixture in a bottle in a dark place and shake it daily, several times if possible, for 14 days. Strain the mixture, bottle it, and keep it in the dark (or use a dark bottle). The normal dosage is 20 to 40 drops, taken two to three times daily. Or use it topically for skin conditions such as athlete's foot or ringworm.

Ratany

Krameria

The shimmering burgundy flowers looked very much like tiny orchids against the dark green of the vine-like leaves. The plant was growing in hot dry sand and seemed not at all bothered. Fortunately, it is not a plant that draws attention and is not often used medically. Although ratany is not endangered, it is not seen frequently.

Medicinal Uses and Preparation

The root is what is usually used medicinally because it has the strongest medical qualities, but the upper part of the plant can also be used. It can be dried and made into a tincture, tea, or ointment.

Ratany is astringent and can be put on injuries to stop bleeding, or on sores and ulcers. In the same way, it can be used as a mouthwash or gargle for a sore mouth or throat. Hemorrhoids have been soothed with the ointment.

Caution

Gather only where there are large numbers of the plants, and please don't pick the last one in the neighborhood. The rule usually followed is to pick no more than one-third of the plants in a colony.

GROWING

This is a questionable plant to grow in the garden; even though it is attractive, it has small burrs for fruit.

178

RATANY TOOTH CLEANER

Dry the ratany root as usual, then powder it. Sprinkle some on a toothbrush, a rag, or a chewed end of a hackberry twig, and clean the teeth. Ratany is good at keeping tartar off the teeth and at tightening the gums (Lesley Bremness, *Herbs*).

Redbud

Cercis canadensis

Redbud is among the first plants to bring color back to the earth after the cold of winter. The flowers come before the full grown foliage and later, the flat, green pods appear, replacing the flowers.

Medicinal Uses and Preparation

The redbud's inner bark and root can be made into a tea or decoction. This was used by different Native American Indian tribes to clear lung congestion, for whooping cough, to prevent nausea and vomiting, and to break fevers. It has also been used for diarrhea, dysentery, and leukemia. The parts can be dried for later use.

Food

The flowers, buds, and young pods have been used for food. The flowers may be eaten raw and make a good nibble on the trail. They are sweet, though the lower part is slightly bitter. The whole flower is somewhat sour. They can be pickled, eaten in salads, or added to bread or pancakes. The young pods can be eaten as a boiled vegetable, stir-fried, sautéed, or even raw.

USED TO TREAT

Diarrhea

Dysentery

Fever

Leukemia

Lung congestion

Nausea

Whooping Cough

Wounds

USED AS/FOR

Antiemetic

Basket weaving

Dye

Food

GROWING

The redbud tree is used extensively in landscaping.

Other Uses

The flowers can be used to make a bright yellow dye with alum as the mordant. The dye is made the same way as sun tea.

The bark has been used by some Native American Indians for weaving baskets.

Current Interest

It makes a good astringent.

Caution

Be moderate in use.

SUN TEA

To make sun tea, place the plant in a glass jar, add water, and place in the sun for several hours. Either fresh or dry herbs can be used.

GARGLE AND WOUND CLEANSER

2 tablespoons of inner bark or root of redbud
3 cups water

Put water and herbs into a pan, and cover. Bring to a boil and simmer 5 minutes. Cover and let sit for 10 minutes.

Strain and use right away or put in a closed container and store in refrigerator not more than 4 to 5 days.

Rose *Rosa*

USED TO TREAT

Backache

Cough

Diarrhea

Dysentery

Fever

Headache

Heart trouble

Nerves

Parasites

Scurvy

Sores

Sore throat

USED AS/FOR

Aromatherapy

Astringent

Food

Potpourri

Tonic

Vitamins

Over one hundred fifty years ago, when the Cherokee still lived in their villages in North Carolina, white men discovered gold on their land and wanted it. Soon they were driven from their homes and marched west from the mountains. This was later called the "Trail of Tears." Men, women, and children; even the old folks and new babies had to leave. Many died and many tears were shed. The women were so sad that the old, wise men gathered one night and asked the Creator to help the women because it was their strength that would help the children—the hope of the new land—to live.

The Creator agreed and, the next day when the women looked back along the trail, they saw that the tears they had shed had turned into small bushes which grew and flowered as they watched. The plant, the Cherokee rose, recovered some of their lost land, and the flowers offered purity in the five creamy white blossoms—even as its brilliant yellow center brought to mind the gold that led the white men to drive them west.

Not only is the rose used as a mild medicine, but the scent of the rose is a relaxant and considered

GROWING

Any type of rose may be grown and used as tea, medicine, or simply to smell or look at. If the wild rose doesn't appeal to you, there are rose varieties to fit every personality, and they are readily available at any nursery.

an aphrodisiac. Cleopatra supposedly had rose petals scattered on the floor about twenty inches deep when Mark Anthony came to visit (Elizabeth Silverthorne, *Legends and Lore of Texas Wildflowers*).

Some of our wild roses, such as the Cherokee rose and the dog rose, can be found in wooded areas, on fence rows, and near old farms. At one time they were used successfully as a fencing. They are often considered pesky and invasive, but their flowers are nice: some are white, others shades of pink.

Medicinal Uses and Preparation

Rose leaves, stems, root, and flowers can be used fresh or dried. Because the hips (the fruit) contain vitamin C, the fresher they are, the better. Rose hips are a treatment for scurvy. Most frequently it is the bark and roots that are made into a decoction. This is a good treatment for dysentery, diarrhea, and worms. It has been used for sore throats, coughs, coughing up blood, and as a wash for sores.

The petals are used in aromatherapy to reduce tension and to calm, and for nervous headaches. In times past, some pregnant women drank rose tea to soothe the unborn baby if it was restless. A tea of leaves and petals is considered useful as a tonic and also as a cold compress to reduce fever. The dried petals are made into a tea for headache, nerves, and heart problems. Add honey in equal amounts with rose water for a cough medicine. Add other parts of the plant if a sore throat is present. A tea made from rose petals and leaves when cooled makes a good compress for headaches.

Food

Rose hip tea tastes much better with a little honey. For another change, add a little rose water. Rose water can be made by placing four ounces of rose petals and two cups of cool water in a canning jar. Seal with the lid and shake the jar. Let it sit for six hours. It can be placed in the refrigerator, but it will not last more than three days. Another method is to set it in the sun as for sun tea. Strength and flavor is a result of the type of rose used. Rose water, either homemade or purchased from a store, can be used in a number of dishes. Whether used to flavor ice cream, sweet rolls, cakes, or frosting, it makes a nice change.

Other Uses

Rose makes good potpourri, beads, sweet-dream pillows, and other love gifts, for in the language of flowers the rose means love.

Current Interest

Rose hips and buds contain a large amount of vitamin C. The plant is high in tannin and makes a good astringent.

A FANTASY JOURNEY WITH ROSES

Set aside a special time for yourself, at least twenty minutes, and fill a tub with tepid bathwater if it is a warm day, or warm water if it is a cold day. Sprinkle liberally with rose petals.

Brew two cups of rose-petal tea with hot water. One cup is for drinking, either hot or cold according to your taste and mood. Add a touch of wild honey. Cool the second cup of tea, then take both cups to the tub. Turn on some mood music, light a candle, and slide in. Soak a cloth with the cool tea—the one without honey—and lay it across your forehead. Lie back and sip the tea and let your mind follow the scent of roses.

A cleansing bath, maybe, but it can't be beat for relaxing, relieving headaches, backaches, anxiety, and frayed nerves.

Sage   *Salvia*

Gil, an Native American Indian healer and a friend, asked me if I'd ever found a man-sage. When I shook my head, he said, "You have to look very carefully to find the man-sage."

"The man-sage?" I asked.

"Yes, he can be recognized by the shape, which is generally that of a man. At times it even seems to be wearing a hat. When gathering sage, watch carefully," he said, "but don't look as if you are interested. If you do, the plant will move because he holds unusual abilities, even intelligence that places it above other plants. It looks much the same as other sage except for its shape.

"Now, the man-sage is sly. If it catches on to the fact that you intend to take him, he will move to another spot, or—will simply disappear.

"That means that you must think ahead and trick it. After discovering him, you must go up casually, paying little attention to him directly, and tie a ribbon or string around him.

"With it tied, he must stay in place. Now comes the hard part. He must be dug up without breaking

USED TO TREAT
Arthritis
Diarrhea
Fever
Headache
Neuralgia
Sore throat
Virus
Wounds
Yeast infection

USED AS/FOR
Antiseptic
Antispasmodic
Food seasoning
Incense
Menstrual regulation
Mouthwash
Tonic

GROWING

Sage may be started from seed, or plants can be bought in most nurseries.

even the tiniest root. The digging must be done with the hands, slowly and carefully to a diameter of ten feet. You must not leave him even if it takes two days. You must sleep beside him but he will probably keep you awake much of the time with dreams or sounds. All this is necessary to take it home. He has unusual powers. I have never seen a man-sage, but I keep looking."

I nodded.

Sage is a most important herb to the Native American Indians as a medicine and for ceremonies and culinary purposes. There are also "sages" that are not true sages but rather members of the *Artemisia* genus, such as mugwort or sagebrush. Sage is a member of the mint family, and as such has a square stem.

Medicinal Uses and Preparation

The genus name *Salvia* carries the idea of health or salvation, and sage was thought to have had the ability to prolong life. It was even claimed in the seventeenth century that use of the herb would render a person immortal.

The leaves have been used for fever and sore throat, colds, headache, arthritis, and neuralgia. Sage decreases secretions of the mouth, sinus, and skin. Considered a general tonic for the blood, sage is found in use from China throughout Europe and the Americas.

This widely distributed plant is reputed to decrease the flow of milk and to aid in weaning babies, human and animal. A sage gargle or mouthwash can be made for the treatment of a sore throat, sore mouth, or gums. After gargling, it should be swallowed. It is reputed to relieve intestinal problems such as diarrhea. Antispasmodic properties have also been attributed to sage. As an antiseptic, it is applied to the skin for hard-to-heal sores or injuries. Other uses include as treatment for menopausal symptoms, menstrual problems, and postpartum cramping.

All parts of the plant may be used, but it is the aerial (aboveground) parts that are most often used. The plant can be dried. The root should be cleaned before drying. Use one teaspoon of dried plant to make tea, which is used for most conditions, even those of the skin. The roots have been boiled and the resulting decoction given to relieve menstrual pain.

Food

Garden sage is a most-recognized plant, and it was brought to the United States from Europe. But many native North American sages are used in all ways.

Current Interest

Recent scientific studies show that the root of certain sages may provide a substitute for tranquilizers. The action decreases anxiety without causing sedation or addiction. Also, it has been found in lab experiments to be effective against yeast and viral diseases such as: *Candida albicans*, the virus of herpes simplex II, the influenza virus A2, the vaccinia virus, and the polio virus II (Michael A. Weiner and Janet A. Weiner, *Herbs That Heal*).

Caution

Although small amounts of sage used in cooking do not cause problems, medicinal doses should not be used by pregnant or nursing mothers. For those with epilepsy, using sage as a medicine could trigger a seizure. Use sage moderately; it can produce symptoms of poisoning (Penelope Ody, *The Complete Medicinal Herbal*).

NATIVE AMERICAN INDIAN USES

Sage is very important in the traditions of most Native American Indian tribes. It is burned in a bundle or container while a person "bathes" in the smoke, which is allowed to continue burning during prayer. This rite is considered an act of purification. Sage is an element in Native American prayer that is much like the Judeo-Christian practice of burning incense.

Sagebrush   *Artemisia*

This tall bushy plant with its gray-green color grows in large colonies throughout the western part of the country. It is similar in looks and smell to sage, but sagebrush is not good to eat. It is very bitter and will ruin food if used as a seasoning.

USED TO TREAT
Arthritis
Diaper rash
Menstrual pain
Parasites
USED AS/FOR
Disinfectant
Insect and mouse repellent
Local anesthetic
Tonic

Medicinal Uses and Preparation

Several *Artemisia* plants provided medicine for both Native American Indians and settlers. Some of these are mugwort, wormwood, and sagebrush. Sagebrush is considered a local anesthetic and is rubbed on the skin for arthritic pains. The dried powdered leaves are used for diaper rash in the Southwest. Sagebrush is a disinfectant and is used to wash and cleanse.

Wormwood, as the name indicates, causes the expulsion of worms from the gastrointestinal tract. Hot wormwood tea is a treatment for painful menstruation. Both true sage (a mint) and wormwood have been used in bitter tonics and are frequently used in the sweat lodge (or sauna), or in the form of smoke for purification by Native American Indians.

Other Uses

The leaves keep bugs such as moths and fleas under control, and sagebrush has been used in the garden to prevent pests from infesting companion plants.

GROWING

Some *Artemisia* are used to advantage in the garden. Most are silver-green and add contrast to other plants.

Caution

In concentrated form, sagebrush can be a narcotic poisoning. Some people may develop a rash after handling the plant; this happened to me. Sagebrush should not be used during pregnancy, or if you have bronchitis or emphysema (Michael Moore, *Los Remedios*).

SAGEBRUSH FIRST-AID

Because sagebrush is so prevalent in the Southwest, it is easy to gather a handful of the leaves and stems, place them in an enamel pan along with water, and boil them. This decoction can be used to treat wounds and as a disinfectant.

When camping in an area where there is sagebrush, lay some branches across fresh food to keep insects and mice (or those ever-present kangaroo rats) away.

Saw Palmetto   *Serenoa repens*

USED TO TREAT

Asthma

Bronchitis

Congestion

Cough

Enlarged prostate

Eye infections

High blood pressure

Migraine

Neuralgia

Snakebite

Sore throat

USED AS/FOR

Aphrodisiac

Breast enlargement

Diuretic

Increasing sperm count

Sedative

Tonic

These small palm trees grow plentifully along the southeastern coast and are found in most parts of Florida and the Gulf Coast. The Indians along these areas knew the medicinal qualities of this plant and used it. There are several species of *Serenoa*, but the small saw palmetto is the best known as a medicine. In the 1870s, reports on its effectiveness began to appear within the contemporary medical community. It was added to the *United States Pharmacopoeia* in 1905.

Medicinal Uses and Preparation

Saw palmetto roots and berries can be dried for later use. They were made into decoctions and tinctures, powdered (berries), and made into tea (apparently least effective).

Native American Indians used the roots for snakebite, sore eyes, and kidney trouble and also as a treatment for high blood pressure and neuralgia. Then as now, the berries were considered an aphrodisiac, not only by the Indians but by many cultures.

In the last century saw palmetto was used to increase sperm count, and to treat inflammation of the bladder (Michael A. Weiner and Janet A. Weiner, *Herbs That Heal*).

GROWING

Many species of *Serenoa* are very popular in landscaping.

The saw palmetto is known as a good tonic and is helpful in treating colds and respiratory problems such as bronchitis, asthma, congestion, irritation of the throat, coughs, and migraine. It has also been used as a sedative and diuretic.

Current Interest

Much research, both in the United States and abroad, has proven that the saw palmetto is effective in relieving enlarged prostates and inflammation, along with the symptoms brought on by these conditions. These tests have shown a decrease of nighttime or frequent urination and an increase of urinary output. There are side effects connected with saw palmetto use in about 5 percent of patients, including diarrhea, constipation, nausea, and other stomach upsets. French and German doctors use saw palmetto regularly as a treatment for enlarged prostate and related symptoms (Michael A. Weiner and Janet A. Weiner, *Herbs That Heal*).

Caution

Rely on professional health-care providers for diagnosis of prostate problems and monitoring of treatment. There are other conditions that may have the same symptoms, or the condition could change into something more serious.

SAW PALMETTO FOR BREAST ENLARGEMENT

During the last century, saw palmetto was used for enlarging the breast. Some herbalists and naturopathic doctors still consider this effective. Because it is not a widespread plant except along the southern coastline, it is usually necessary to buy the capsules or extracts (James A. Duke, *The Green Pharmacy*).

Self-heal

Prunella vulgaris

USED TO TREAT

Bites

Boils

Bruises

Burns

Diarrhea

Headache

Parasites

Scrapes

Sore throat

Stomachache

USED AS/FOR

Antispasmodic

Astringent

Disinfectant

Energy

Menstrual regulation

Mouthwash

Sedative

At one time this timid plant was considered an important herb, and although its popularity has decreased, it is worth remembering. It blends into its surroundings until it blooms, then it becomes a show-off. Its purple-pink flowers can be seen easily, and it is a natural for planting. The plants grow from six to eight inches in height.

Medicinal Uses and Preparation

Self-heal, or heal-all, is a transplant from Europe, but it has become naturalized in the United States and is to be found scattered throughout most of the country. It was used by very early settlers and later by Native American Indians for many of the same things. All above-ground parts of the plant are useful. It can be used fresh, or dried for later use. Make it into a tincture, an infusion, or an ointment for topical use following the basic directions in the Gathering and Preparation chapter.

Self-heal is astringent and helps to stop bleeding. It is a first-aid in the case of wounds—a tea could be used in this case. It has been used to decrease menstrual flow and to treat bites, burns, and boils. Other uses of self-heal are to help cure diarrhea, mouth sores, scrapes, bruises, an

GROWING

The roots spread underground and shoot up, forming new plants. These can be separated and transplanted. Self-heal is very pretty when blooming, and colonies growing along roadsides add color to the spring flower mix. Self-heal can be started from seed, but this method is not certain. The plant is handled by some nurseries.

Other common names are sicklewort and woundwort. The plant has a terminal fat spike with flowers growing near the top.

upset stomach, and worms. It can also be used as a gargle for sore throats or mouths.

The tea or a tincture might also be given to calm someone who is upset, or to someone with a headache. Along the same line, it is used with hyperactive children. Heal-all is also considered an anti-spasmodic.

The leaves can be made into a poultice for simple scrapes or bruises, and placing damp leaves of the plant on the eyes and fore-head is thought to relieve tiredness. It has been used to increase energy.

Current Interest

Self-heal contains substances that are diuretic and act against tumors. Lab tests indicate it may also be antibiotic, hypotensive, and antimutagenic in action (Steven Foster and James A. Duke, *Eastern/Central Medicinal Plants*).

Caution

Although self-heal has the ability to stop bleeding, any abnormal or heavy bleeding should be checked out by a medical professional.

MOUTHWASH OR GARGLE

1-½ tablespoons of fresh self-heal or 1 heaping teaspoon of the dried herb
1 cup very hot water

Place the herb in a pot or cup, pour the hot water over it, cover, and let it steep for 10 to 15 minutes. Use this mouth-wash or gargle three to four times a day, including at bed-time.

Senna *Cassia marilandica*

This was one of the herbs my Cherokee grandmother raised in her garden. My mother remembered taking doses of senna tea. My grandmother treated any stomachache, fever, and most other common symptoms of children with this tea. Mama would never drink hot tea of any kind because it reminded her of this medicine.

Wild senna is native to North America and as such was much used by Native American Indians and settlers.

Medicinal Uses and Preparation

The leaves are gathered while the plant is blooming, then are dried. The roots can be used fresh or dried.

Senna has been used as a purgative and to cause vomiting. If a milder action is needed, try using the seed pods instead of the leaf in making the tea.

Tea made from the roots was given for heart trouble, cramps, and fever. Root poultices for sores were made by digging the root, making a decoction, putting the pulp between two cloths, and laying it on the sore area. Senna has also been used as a diuretic, to get rid of worms, and as mouthwash.

USED TO TREAT

Cramps

Constipation

Fever

Heart trouble

Parasites

Sores

USED AS/FOR

Diuretic

Emetic

Mouthwash

GROWING

Senna is found in the eastern half of the United States and can be grown in this region. Plants can be found in native-plant nurseries, or they may be grown from seed.

Current Interest

Pharmaceutical medicines are made from an imported form of senna, but the action is basically the same as with the native variety. It is usually intended for laxative use.

Caution

Nursing mothers should not take senna because it finds its way into mother's milk, and babies will be affected.

A LAXATIVE TEA

1 scant teaspoon senna leaf
½ teaspoon fresh or dry ginger
1 cup very hot water

Put the herbs in a cup and add the hot water. Steep for 30 minutes.

Shepherd's Purse *Capsella bursa-pastoris*

USED TO TREAT

Cystitis

Diarrhea

High blood pressure

Malaria

Nosebleed

Parasites

Poison ivy

USED AS/FOR

Astringent

Contraction stimulation

Diuretic

Food

Quinine substitute

Sometimes there is a plant so insignificant-looking that even those who should know better turn aside without a second look. Shepherd's purse, also known as St. James wort and mother's hearts, is just such a plant. It has tiny white flowers on top of a stem with heart-shaped pods below, and the stem reaches down into a basal rosette of toothed leaves. The base may be six inches in diameter with the top of the stem no more than twelve inches in height and often smaller. But don't be fooled—those little plants are powerful and hold a wealth of medicinal value.

Medicinal Uses and Preparation

The upper part of the plant is used fresh and can be dried for later use. One of the properties of the plant is to stop bleeding. It does this by contracting the veins, which makes it useful in the treatment of varicose veins and bleeding. Nosebleed has been treated by wetting a piece of cotton with the tea and putting it in the nose. It has been used during childbirth by folk healers to stimulate contractions both before the birth and afterward. It also helps postpartum bleeding.

It is used against tumors and has been taken in place of quinine for malaria. Shepherd's purse was used by the

GROWING

It isn't likely this little plant will be found in a nursery, but if you watch your garden, it may just show up. If you're in a hurry, take a walk to the next street or vacant lot and you can probably gather seeds or even a plant to transplant. There is no danger of extinction.

Native American Indians in cases of diarrhea, poison ivy, worms, and stomach problems. It has been made into a poultice for bleeding wounds. It temporarily lowers blood pressure. One of the main uses of the plant is for cystitis, and it will also act as a diuretic.

Food

The very young leaves may be used fresh as a salad or cooked with greens or soups. Shepherd's purse has a spicy flavor, and removing the purses and sprinkling them on soups or salad provides seasoning similar to pepper.

Current Interest

Shepherd's purse has been shown to have antitumor properties and is anti-inflammatory. In the lab it has been found to prevent duodenal ulcers from forming in rats under stress, and it inhibits the growth of bacteria. Tests have also proven it stops bleeding internally, including uterine bleeding.

Caution

Avoid taking shepherd's purse during pregnancy because it stimulates uterine contractions. The seed can cause skin blisters in some sensitive people.

Skullcap   *Scutellaria*

USED TO TREAT

Depression

Diarrhea

High blood
pressure

Hysteria

Neuralgia

USED AS/FOR

Antiseptic

Antispasmodic

Sedative

Tonic

One species of skullcap has a history of being a cure for hydrophobia and is called maddog weed. It is a member of the mint family and has a square stem and often grows near water. The leaves are similar to those of other mints, as are the purple to lavender flowers. Some plants grow tall and some are short. The blooms are different from other blossoms in that the top part of the flower resembles a hood.

One species, *S. drummondii*, is very distinctive. The purple flowers have two long white spots on the lower lips, and these spots are dotted with purple. Some claim this plant is a good medicine plant, but there are also those who claim it to have poisonous qualities. Don't take any chances. Consult with someone who is knowledgeable in using herbal medicine before deciding to use skullcap.

Medicinal Uses and Preparation

The plant may be dried, crushed, and stored in an airtight container. Use one teaspoon of leaves to eight ounces of hot water. Make an infusion and strain. Use two tablespoons as needed. A tincture may also be made from fresh

GROWING

Skullcap makes a very pretty garden plant. It grows in clumps, topped with bright violet-blue flowers.

or dried leaves. Use twenty drops several times a day. This can be added to juice or other liquid if preferred.

Skullcap has been used as an antispasmodic and for anxiety, hysteria, depression, and neuralgia. It has been used in the case of convulsions.

The Cherokees have used it for diarrhea and kidney problems (Paul B. Hamel and Mary U. Chiltoskey, *Cherokee Plants—Their Uses: A 400-Year-Old History*).

Current Interest

One skullcap species, *S. baicalensis*, from China, has been shown to lower blood pressure. Another species, *S. barbata*, is useful against certain cancer cells (Lesley Bremness, *Herbs*).

Caution

Overuse may cause jitters or restlessness. Toxicity is unknown; however, *S. drummondii* is considered by some to be poisonous.

A RELAXING TEA

½ teaspoon dried skullcap
½ teaspoon dried Passionflower vine
1 teaspoon rose syrup
1 cup boiling water

Put the herbs in a pot and pour in the boiling water. Cover and steep for 10 minutes. Add the rose syrup. Drink hot or add ice. This is a good tea to offer for depression, anxiety, or just an inability to relax.

Soapberry   *Sapindus Drummondii*

The soapberry looks similar to the chinaberry tree in its leaves, shape, and fruit, but a closer look shows that the leaves and berries are slightly different. The fruit is translucent, and the black shiny seeds can be seen in them as if through smoke. When in fruit it can be heavy with the berries and is very attractive. It is also somewhat medicinal and useful.

USED TO TREAT

Arthritis

Cough

Fever

USED AS/FOR

Anti-inflammatory

Soap

Medicinal Uses and Preparation

Use dried leaves and stems that have been gathered in late summer or early fall. A cold infusion can be made from the dried herb. This is used for dry coughs, fevers, some kidney disorders, inflammation, and acute arthritis pain.

Other Uses

The berries can be crushed and used as laundry soap. They can be preserved for use in shampoo and hand soap in a tincture.

Caution

The soapberry should be used only over the short term.

When using the soap, it might be wise to do a skin test on the inner arm, because some people are sensitive

GROWING

The soapberry has recently been used in landscaping. Check for it in native-plant nurseries. If it is not available, a few berries, each containing one large seed, would supply you with a beginning.

to it. Use the preserved soap or fresh berry juice in the evening and leave it on the arm until the next morning.

TO MAKE SOAP

The soapberry berries should be mashed and the seeds removed, then the juice should be strained. The juice can be used as is for washing clothes.

To make a preserved soap for hands and hair, start with ½ cup of strained juice (approximately 4–6 cups of berries) and add ¼ cup of Everclear. Seal the liquid in a canning jar or similar airtight container. Allow it to sit for 10 days and it is ready for use. Be sure to do a skin test before using the soap.

Soapwort   *Saponaria officinalis*

A plant brought to this country by early European settlers, soapwort, or bouncing Bet, is a favorite of gardeners. It has naturalized in the United States and was incorporated easily into Native American Indian life.

Medicinal Uses and Preparation

Historically, soapwort has been used as a laxative or blood tonic, as an expectorant, to help with gout and rheumatism, leprosy, asthma, gallbladder and liver disease, and venereal disease. Topically, it has been used for eczema, acne, and psoriasis. Native American Indians used soapwort for poulticing boils, to treat poison oak rash, and as a laxative. Soap is prepared by boiling the leaves and roots in water. The leaves may also be crushed and mixed with water for a first-aid cleanser or soap.

Food

The flowers may be added to salads.

Other Uses

Soapwort has been used in brewing to add a head to beer. It is used extensively by conservators for cleaning delicate materials and metals such as pewter.

USED TO TREAT
Acne
Asthma
Boils
Constipation
Dandruff
Eczema
Gout
Poison oak
Psoriasis
Rheumatism
Venereal disease

USED AS/FOR
Beer brewing
Blood tonic
Expectorant
Soap

GROWING
The plant is available in nurseries. Seed may also be bought.

202

Research is being done to study the effect of the plant on breast cancer and leukemia.

Use caution in taking soapwort internally. Overuse may cause poisoning. Soapwort should not be taken during pregnancy.

SOAPWORT TEA AND DECOCTION

When making soapwort tea, use ½ ounce of the leaves. Pour 2 cups of boiling water over the leaves, cover, and steep for 20 minutes. Strain the tea and store it in the refrigerator. Use within 2 days.

To use the root, put 1 teaspoon of the herb in 2 cups of cool water and cover. Bring to a boil, reduce the heat, and simmer for 30 minutes. Turn off the heat and cool the liquid while it is covered. This decoction is used for cleansing, poultices, as a dandruff treatment, and as soap for sensitive skin.

Spiderwort Commelinaceae

The bright blue to purple (occasionally white) spiderworts of the *Tradescantia* genus are among the first flowers to bloom in the spring. From a base of wide grasslike leaves a stalk shoots up, holding the blossom of three petals. Another plant, the dayflower (*Commelina*) is very similar; however, it blooms through to fall. It has only two blue petals and a small white one below. Both plants are edible. Spiderwort is found in the eastern United States and in the South and Southwest.

USED TO TREAT

Bites and stings

Constipation

Stomachache

USED AS/FOR

Food

Medicinal Uses and Preparation

Spiderwort has been used by Cherokees to aid in the relief of stings and bug bites. It was crushed and rubbed on the skin. It was mixed with other ingredients for other problems such as kidney and female problems. A tea was made for pain and upset stomach, and as a laxative. The roots were used to make a poultice that was used for cancer (Paul B. Hamel and Mary U. Chiltoskey, *Cherokee Plants—Their Uses: A 400-Year-Old History*).

Food

The thick upper part of the plants may be eaten raw, as in salads, or cooked. The young stems, with the leaves, may

GROWING

Spiderwort plants are frequently found in general plant nurseries because they are frequently used in landscaping. They are easy to grow and multiply quickly, especially in shade with moisture.

be gathered, broken into pieces, and boiled until just tender. Butter and serve. It is at this point you'll understand, if one of your kids hasn't pointed it out, why spiderwort is sometimes called snot weed. Older stems may be tough but not distasteful, and leaves are tender at any stage.

The flowers may be candied like borage. Brush the flowers with egg white, roll them in sugar, and dry. Because the flowers wilt quickly, pick and coat them one at a time.

Caution

The roots of spiderwort may contain poisons. Eat only the upper part of the plant.

NATURAL RADIATION DETECTOR

Spiderworts have been found to demonstrate certain changes when exposed to nuclear radiation. The stamen hairs change from blue to pink, and the amount of exposure is reflected in the number of cells that have changed when the plant is studied under a microscope (Reader's Digest, *Magic and Medicine of Plants*).

Stonecrop

Sedum

Stonecrop is not seen as an individual plant but as a giant carpet of yellow and green that may suddenly cover rocky dry ground. I have been down a road where no flowers grew only to come back over a short time and find this colorful succulent carpeting the earth. It is especially heartening to see this when the climate is so hot and dry that everything else around is wilted or dying. Maybe one of stonecrop's common names came from this: Live forever. It is known in Mexico as "síempreviva."

Medicinal Uses and Preparation

Most of the time stonecrop is used fresh. Poultices of stonecrop have been made and applied to sores and boils. It has been crushed and warmed for a poultice to treat pain in the back. The juice may be used for sores and wounds because it is considered a good antiseptic. The plant is also laxative in action. Stonecrop has been used for the removal of warts and corns.

Food

Stonecrop leaves and stems can be eaten raw or cooked. The dried leaves have been used as a spice. It might be wise not to eat too much at one time because stonecrop is also an emetic.

USED TO TREAT

Backache

Boils

Constipation

Corns

High blood pressure

Sores

Warts

USED AS/FOR

Antiseptic

GROWING

The plant grows over much of the United States and needs little water. It makes a good cover crop, especially in dry areas of sand and around stones and graveled spots. It may be transplanted, but some species are rare.

Current Interest

The leaves and stems of stonecrop can lower blood pressure, and the juice works against bacteria.

With the antiseptic, healing, and soothing properties stonecrop has, one questions whether it might be useful in healing ulcers and mouth sores.

Caution

There are some people who might have reactions to stonecrop. If trying it for the first time, use only a small amount at first. This is a good idea with any herb.

STONECROP SURVIVAL

Stonecrop stores water in its leaves much as the *Aloe vera* does, consequently, it can last longer than other plants. But that's not all. This plant has a back-up system that gives it an even greater chance of survival. The pores of the wax-coated leaves are kept closed during the day to prevent the loss of moisture, and at night they open to absorb carbon dioxide, a necessity for the growth of the plant (Reader's Digest, *Magic and Medicine of Plants*).

Sumac

Rhus

USED TO TREAT

Angina

Asthma

Boils

Diarrhea

Earache

Fever

Gonorrhea

Hemorrhoids

Kidney stones

Menstrual pain

Poison oak

Sore throat

Stomachache

Tobacco
addiction

Toothache

Tuberculosis

Wounds

USED AS/FOR

Astringent

Diuretic

Food

Mouthwash

Stimulation of
milk flow

Colorful fall leaves lining country roads may be painted by oak, aspen, maple, or even mesquite, but more than likely, sumac is a part of the show. Those with fire-colored leaves and bunches of bright red fruit can't help but be noticed. Like many wild plants, sumac is looked upon as a pest by many, though others are glad for its presence. This group of small trees was among the most used among Native American Indians and settlers alike, and it is still an important medicine plant.

There are many species, but, generally the actions are similar, and all sumacs have red berries. This makes it easy to recognize poison sumac: It has white berries.

Medicinal Uses and Preparation

Sumac berries should be red when gathered. The leaves can be gathered at any stage. It is easy to hang up a whole stem with fruit or lay leaves or fruit on paper to dry. The leaves will be effective for a year, and the berries will last two to three years (Michael Moore, *Medicinal Plants of the Desert and Canyon West*).

Tea for medicinal purposes may be made from one teaspoon of red berries, fresh or dry, in five cups of water.

GROWING

The bushes can be grown from seed or bought from native-plant nurseries. Sumac is found growing wild across the United States.

Bring to a boil and simmer for thirty minutes, cover, and let the tea stand until it is cool. Drink one swallow when needed, up to one to two cups per day (Michael A. Weiner and Janet A. Weiner, *Herbs That Heal*).

One of the main active ingredients of the sumac is tannin, and for this reason, it works as an astringent. The tea is used as a wash. It works well as a gargle for sore mouth, gums, or throat. The tea is also taken for diarrhea, tuberculosis, and angina. It has been used to treat cancer, as a stomach tonic, and as a diuretic. There are reports that it works well against gonorrhea. It is said to aid in urinary problems, stomachache, and painful menstruation, to stimulate milk flow, to remove kidney stones, and to treat fever and earache.

The leaves can be dried and powdered to be used when needed. The powder can be made into a salve, tincture, or used as is. If the tincture is diluted it can even be made into a nose spray for irritation.

The leaves have been used as a poultice for boils, cuts, wounds, ulcers, old sores, and poison oak. They stanch bleeding and shrink hemorrhoids. The leaves and berries have been smoked for asthma, and the berries have been considered a cure for tobacco addiction when smoked. The fruit is also used for toothache and, when made into ear drops, for earache.

The dried, sifted, and powdered leaves can be used directly on minor cuts to stop bleeding. Always store dried herbs in an airtight container.

Food

Rhusade can be made with one cup cool water and one tablespoon berries, either fresh or dried. Let set about fifteen to twenty minutes, strain and sweeten, then add ice. Bruise the berries a little to hasten the brew. This beverage tea is not made with hot water to prevent the release of the tannin, which might make it bitter.

Dried crushed berries can also be sprinkled on meat for flavor.

Other Uses

Reportedly, sumac can be used to make a fast dye to color fabric from pale brown to dark brown. The tannin acts as a mordant to make the color last.

Sumac's tannin content, with its astringent effect, is used as a mouthwash and gargle for sore mouths and throats. It will also stop bleeding.

Caution

Some people are highly sensitive to sumac and may have a reaction to it similar to a poison oak rash. Poison sumac, which is a smaller plant than most sumacs and has white fruit, will cause poison oak–like reactions. Do not use this for medicine or to eat.

GLYCERINE PREPARATION OF SUMAC

5 grams (by weight) dried and powdered sumac leaves
4 ounces glycerine
2 ounces distilled water

Mix all ingredients together and store in a dark place. Shake the mixture frequently, at least once a day, for 14 days. Strain the liquid and bottle it in dark bottles or store in the dark.

This preparation is to be used on sore mucous membranes such as lips, mouth, and genitals (Michael Moore, *Medicinal Plants of the Desert and Canyon West*).

NAVAJO SAUCE

In New Mexico, the Navajo use the berries of three-leaved sumac for cooking. The fruit is put into bread or made into a sauce after the berries are gathered and ground fine.

I helped some friends with this one day. We ground 2 cups of the fruit in a coffee grinder. We put it into a pan with 3/4 cup sugar and enough water to almost cover it. This was cooked while we stirred constantly until it was thick. It was delicious over ice cream.

Sunflower   *Helianthus*

Sunflowers are native to the Americas and common throughout the United States. Depending on the soil and moisture and species, they may reach more than six feet high or no more than a foot. The leaves may be as large as twelve by eighteen inches. The leaves are dark green, rough with toothed edges, and have stiff hairs along the underside and down the stem. Inside the stem is a pithy core.

Medicinal Uses and Preparation

This core is referred to in *The Dispensatory of the United States*. The pith was taken and rolled into a small cylinder and wrapped tightly with cotton and covered with muslin. It was lit and put against the skin as close to the area of pain as possible, and was used in cases of deafness, asthma, muscular weakness, and a diseased spine, to name a few. This was a routine treatment for chronic complaints. It wasn't too smart to worry the doctor over trivial health problems at that time—he might try and burn them out. Some Native American Indian tribes used the pith in much the same way.

The seeds are used as an expectorant for coughs, as a diuretic, for kidney disease, and diarrhea. They have also been used to treat fevers and malaria. The dried plant may

USED TO TREAT
Arthritis
Boils
Diabetes
Diarrhea
Fever
Malaria
Snakebite
Spider bites
USED AS/FOR
Diuretic
Expectorant
Food

GROWING

Sunflowers are easy to grow, and the seeds are easily obtained from any store that sells seed. They need little care and produce nice backgrounds in the garden. Jerusalem artichoke is grown from tubers and is sold at nurseries that specialize in native American plants.

211

be steeped and the tea put in bathwater for relief of arthritis. The leaves have been made into a poultice for snakebite or spider bites, boils, and lung ailments. Tea made from the above-ground parts of the plant have been used as a diuretic and expectorant.

Food

Energy cakes made of the seeds of sunflower were made for Native American Indian warriors to eat on the trail so they wouldn't have to stop to fix a meal. The seeds are high in protein, minerals, calcium, and potassium. They also contain vitamins A, B complex, and some E.

Cooking oil may be obtained from crushing the seeds, boiling them, then skimming the oil from the water. Ground toasted seeds make a good flour. To make a coffeelike beverage, toast the seeds, grind the shells, and brew.

Jerusalem artichoke (*Helianthus tuberosus*) is a cousin of the common sunflower. It has a much smaller flower with seeds of no consequence, but below the ground the plant produces a tuber that is very much like a potato. It can be eaten raw, boiled, fried, and any way a potato may be eaten. It can be added to soup or stew and used like water chestnuts. These sunflowers are prolific producers, and the tubers, shaped like small knotty potatoes, keep in a cool place for months. The Maximilian sunflower (*Helianthus Maximiliani*) produces smaller tubers that may be used similarly.

Current Interest

The tubers of Jerusalem artichokes contain insulin, and in folk medicine it has been used for diabetes.

Caution

Some people may be allergic to sunflower pollen or the plant extract.

A TREATMENT FOR MALARIA

Many countries now grow sunflowers, and Russia is especially fond of them. This treatment for malaria is practiced there.

Lay a large cloth across a bed. Place sunflower leaves over this and sprinkle them with warm milk. Place the patient on this and wrap him up. This will cause him to sweat. This treatment is continued each day until the fever breaks (William H. Hylton, *The Rodale Herb Book*).

Teasel

Dipsacus

It was hard to tell what it was, but the stickery little weed seemed worthless and maybe even malicious. Then I remembered another plant that came to my garden and that I pulled up in a panic, only to find later that it would have been useful. Give this one a chance, I thought. It can always be pulled, but I can't put it back.

The weed grew fast, and every day it was taller. My hand still wanted to reach out and jerk it up, but my reason prevailed. Then it got interesting. The long pointed leaves that grew opposite one another grew around to catch and fuse, forming a little cup around the thick prickly stem. At the top was a large burr. It rained and water stayed in the cup. The stem grew taller, and more leaves clasped one another. Then new stems formed, and new heads. The plant continued to grow and form new branches. Now the top burr, the shape of an egg and about the same size, has reached my nose and has a pale violet fringe of flowers about the middle. This is definitely a special plant, and I won't dig it up at all. This prickly growth crept into the United States long ago, just as it crept into my garden several weeks ago.

USED TO TREAT

Blackheads

Eye infection

Indigestion

Jaundice

Warts

Wrinkles

USED AS/FOR

Anti-inflammatory

Appetite stimulant

Diaphoretic

Menstrual regulation

GROWING

This is not a plant you'd want thickets of, but a plant or two are certainly eye-catching because of their size, overall shape, and the interesting leaf cups.

🌱 213

Medicinal Uses and Preparation

The root of teasel is the part that is medicinal, and it is considered good medicine for the liver, treating jaundice, helping get rid of excess fluid, and eliminating warts and blackheads.

Teasel root has also been used in cases of infection, to aid indigestion, as an appetite stimulant, for sties, skin inflammation, the regulation of menses, to bring about sweating, and for cancer.

Other Uses

Teasel was once grown as a crop to provide the burrs that were used to comb woolens.

The seed heads blend in well with other dried plants for floral arrangements.

Current Interest

Except in folk medicine, teasel is seldom used. Even its use in industry is limited: Most manufacturers now use man-made combs, and teasel burrs see only specialized use.

GYPSY USE OF TEASEL

The water collected from the pockets formed by the leaves of the teasel was used by gypsies as a face treatment for wrinkles, irritated eyes, and to get rid of dark circles under the eyes (Lesley Bremness, *Herbs*).

Trumpet Vine   *Campsis*

Trumpet vine or trumpet creeper is native to the South but has made its way across the United States. The heavy green vine is perennial and has large bright red-orange trumpet flowers.

Medicinal Uses and Preparation

The fresh plant can be irritating to the hands, but drying eliminates this. Dry all parts of the plant and make a basic tea for treatments of fungus, yeast, and tinea infections. It can be used as a douche for candida (Michael Moore, *Medicinal Plants of the Desert and Canyon West*).

Caution

Some people may be sensitive to the fresh plant. Wear gloves when gathering trumpet vine.

USED TO TREAT

Fungus infections

Yeast infections

USED AS/FOR

Douche

BODY POWDER FOR INFECTIONS

Using dried trumpet vine, a powder can be made for the skin to treat fungus or tinea infections (Michael Moore, *Medicinal Plants of the Desert and Canyon West*).

Many times in older persons who are inactive, infections grow in the folds of the skin and under the breasts. A damp warm environment increases the risk of this kind of infection. It might be worth giving this simple powder a try.

GROWING

The plant can be grown from seed or the root. It is very invasive. It might be worth having in spite of that; certainly many people think so.

Vervain

Verbena

USED TO TREAT

Depression

Diarrhea

Gout

Headache

Hemorrhoids

Insomnia

Menstrual pain

Nerves

Stomachache

Wounds

USED AS/FOR

Antispasmodic

Appetite suppressant

Astringent

Contraception

Digestion

Diuretic

Emetic

Hair growth

Sedative

Stimulation of milk flow

Vervain is considered a mystical plant throughout the world. Some Native American Indian tribes look on it as magical. Vervain was placed on the altars in ancient Rome, was used to repel witches in England, and is considered to have special powers (the power to heal and assist with women's conditions and childbirth) in this country. It is little wonder this plant is considered to be more than medicine.

Medicinal Uses and Preparation

Vervain should be picked while it is in bloom. It is easily tied in bundles and hung to dry. A tea can then be made of it. Adding mint, lemon balm, or another tasty herb along with a little honey might make it easier to drink, for vervain tea is bitter.

The tea is taken for menstrual cramps, to stimulate the flow of mother's milk, and has also been used for contraception. A tea of vervain was often used to provide sedation in the case of nervousness and tension that might be indicated by depression, headache, or sleeplessness. Vervain was considered antispasmodic and good for digestion, stomach problems, diarrhea, and pain in the bladder or during urination. It is also diuretic and was thought to be a good treatment for the gallbladder and the liver.

GROWING

The plant is grown by seeds or root division. It is a small plant with attractive blue flowers. Some species are leafy and have thick spikes, whereas others are thin with a more miniature flower. In either case, the flowers can be used along the edges of a garden to good advantage.

The tea was said to promote hair growth. Vervain is astringent and is used as a poultice for wounds, hemorrhoids, skin ulcers, and tumors. It has also been used as an emetic, to bring on vomiting.

Other Uses

Vervain has been used as a good luck charm, protection against witches, and to fan the flame of love.

Current Interest

Early tests indicate that vervain could be used for heart problems and tumors. It is effective as a diuretic, helps decrease appetite, and relieves gout.

Caution

Vervain should not be used during pregnancy.

LOVE POTIONS

Ever wonder how a love potion was made? Here's an example. The ingredients below are listed with their "love properties."

A small acacia flower for a sweet love.

A small leaf of sage to attract.

A medium leaf of mint to ensure faith.

Two rose petals for pure love.

The flowering end of vervain of the size of the first joint of the little finger for long-lasting love.

After choosing the right balance of ingredients, the person making the potion might brew the mix into a tea, adding a little honey for sweetness, and exchange it for a bit of silver. It was that simple—and probably very profitable.

Violet

Viola

USED TO TREAT

Bites

Bronchitis

Constipation

Cough

Diaper rash

Diarrhea

Eczema

Fever

Headache

Insomnia

Lung congestion

Sores

Varicose veins

USED AS/FOR

Blood tonic

Eyewash

Food

Mouthwash

Perfume

Potpourri

Vitamins

Long ago, Venus asked her son Cupid to choose who, among herself and a group of young women, was the most beautiful. When he chose the young women, his mother was so furious that she struck the women until they were blue and continued to do so until they had shriveled into violets at her feet.

The violet is an ancient plant that has figured into many myths, like the one above. Perfume, foods, and medicine are all provided by the violet. This little plant, which keeps close to the ground, is certainly not much used and is often dug as a pest. Pliny spoke of violets being steeped in vinegar and taken for gout. He also suggested that a chaplet of the flowers would get rid of a headache (Reader's Digest, *Magic and Medicine of Plants*).

There are many different common names for the various violets, such as sweet violet, woods violet, and johnny-jump-up, also known as heartsease.

Medicinal Uses and Preparation

The leaves and flowers can be used fresh and dried. The plant contains ingredients similar to aspirin. Flowers have been boiled and made into eyewash.

GROWING

Violets grow in partial sun. They are considered woodland flowers. Some species may need some protection, but I've found violets to be very invasive. The seed can be planted during the fall, and the roots or plants may be transplanted.

The flower syrup may be used for fragile capillaries, coughs, headaches, sleeplessness, as a mild laxative, and to stimulate circulation. Flowers and leaves can usually be used interchangeably or together to make tea or a decoction. Such has been used for rheumatism, varicose veins, to stimulate circulation, to strengthen capillaries, and as a gargle.

A tea of the leaves is used for diarrhea. It has been applied to diaper rash, sores, bites, skin ulcers, and eczema. Poultices have also been used for such conditions. Both leaf and flower tea have been used as a blood tonic and to help with urinary problems.

The leaves may be poulticed on the head for headache. Perhaps, at the same time, taking a teaspoon of flower syrup or a cool violet drink would add to the effectiveness of the poultice.

Violet roots have been made into a decoction or tea for bronchitis, cancer, fevers, and lung problems (it works as a decongestant).

Food

Violets contain vitamin C and more vitamin A than carrots. One-half cup of leaves provides more than the minimum daily requirement of vitamin A. The plants can be cooked with other greens or alone.

The flowers can be made into jelly, jam, syrup, or violet water. They can be made into candy, or the flowers may be candied for garnish. Use only the blue flowers, not yellow or white (Delena Tull, *A Practical Guide to Edible and Useful Plants*).

Other Uses

Violets are used in perfumes, potpourri, and many handicrafts.

Current Interest

Studies have shown that there is a possibility of antitumor action in the violet, and it may also be effective for skin problems.

Caution

Violets offer no real problem except that the seeds and roots can cause vomiting in some people or when a high dose is taken.

African violets are not kin to the wild violets and should not be eaten.

VIOLET SYRUP

½ cup violet flowers, packed
½ cup water

Place the flowers and water in a canning jar, seal, and leave in the refrigerator for 24 hours. Strain the liquid.

Add 1 cup of honey to the violet water. You may add 1 teaspoon lemon juice (optional). Put the liquid in a stainless steel or graniteware pan and bring it to a boil. Immediately after the boil, cut the fire and pour the hot syrup into a sterile jar and seal.

The syrup may be used undiluted as a cough syrup, as a treatment for headache, fragile capillaries, cough, or may be added to ice water for a cool, refreshing drink.

Watercress *Nasturtium officinale*

The Cherokee mother walked to the edge of the water carrying her sick child. It was cold as she stepped in it, but that didn't matter. She moved to a deeper spot and dipped the little one beneath the water four times. He caught his breath each time but made no cry. Then she went toward the bank, where plants were floating near the edge. She picked a plant, thanked it for its help, and put some in the child's mouth. He looked at her and chewed greedily. She wrapped a blanket around both and moved down the path, assured the baby would now be cured.

Watercress grows in cold flowing water and has the common name of scurvy grass. Although its scientific genus name is *Nasturtium*, it is not kin to the garden flower. The taxonomic name of that plant is *Tropaeolum majus*.

Medicinal Uses and Preparation

Watercress is high in vitamin C and is a good treatment and preventative for scurvy. The lime content in watercress is high enough to be beneficial to those with "soft" teeth and bones.

USED TO TREAT
Bronchitis
Gallstones
Goiters
Lethargy
Nerves
Rheumatism
Scurvy

USED AS/FOR
Blood purification
Diuretic
Food seasoning
Hair growth
Skin conditioner
Vitamins

GROWING
Because watercress grows in cool flowing water, it is necessary to reproduce the same conditions to cultivate it.

221

The plant is a blood cleanser, works as a diuretic, and helps in kidney problems. It contains iodine and therefore is used to treat goiters. The plant is given for colds, bronchitis, and other respiratory infections. An ointment containing watercress was once used to treat sword wounds.

Nervousness and rheumatism have both been treated with watercress. The tea has even been given for heart problems, lethargy, gallstones, and hair loss. Another treatment for hair loss is to rub the juice of the plant on the head.

Food

Watercress has a tangy, peppy flavor that is good in salads, soups, sandwiches, and is attractive as a garnish. It is rich in vitamins C, A, B, and E, iron, copper, iodine, and magnesium, and is high in calcium.

Other Uses

Watercress is prepared as a skin conditioner.

Current Interest

According to Lesley Bremness in her book *Herbs*, "the juice dissolves nicotine."

Caution

Wild watercress plants may have harmful germs or parasites, including liver flukes. Wash wild plants thoroughly before eating or, better yet, cook the plant to make sure it is safe.

Watercress should not be taken every day, nor should it be taken over a long period of time. Even with intermittent treatment, it can cause kidney irritation. Neither should the undiluted juice be drunk, because it can cause inflammation of the throat and stomach (John Lust, *The Herb Book*).

ECZEMA TREATMENT

1 tablespoon chopped watercress
1 cup hot water (not boiling)

Steep for 10 minutes, then allow to cool. Use about ¼ cup of the strained tea to pat on the face or other affected area. Drink the other part of the tea.

Water Lily

Nelumbo luteam,
Nuphar luteum,
Nymphaea odorata

Who can resist the charm of water lilies? Even the Latin name of some bring to mind the nymphs who lived in ancient mythology. Pretty to look at, nice to smell, but did you ever think of eating them or using them for medicine? Well, both have been done, and with good results. Not only do the rocking of the pads and the swaying of the flowers have a relaxing effect, but some have a perfume that delivers another healing touch to the senses.

All of the water lilies listed above are similar in their uses. The yellow lotus, *Nelumbo lutea*, has leaves up to twenty-four inches in diameter. Its green leaf either lies flat or grows above the water. Sometimes it looks like an umbrella turning inside out. Inside the flower is a cuplike seedpod with little mounds on its flat surface. As these mature the yellow petals drop off, and the pod looks something like a salt or pepper shaker.

Spatterdock, *Nuphar luteum*, has leaves that are round and notched. These sometimes grow above the

USED TO TREAT
Boils
Bruises
Cough
Diarrhea
Infected glands
Mouth ulcers
Sore throat
Tuberculosis
Wounds
Yeast infections
USED AS/FOR
Anti-inflammatory
Astringent
Food
Insect repellent
Perfume
Reducing sex drive

GROWING

It is necessary to have some type of water available, such as a lily pond, cow tank, or a slow-moving stream, in order to grow these plants. There are, however, specialized nurseries that have all the equipment and plants necessary to set up your own water garden.

 223

water. The flower gives the impression of never quite opening. It is round, and the petals barely show themselves. It is also known as the yellow pond lily.

The fragrant white water lily, *Nymphaea odorata,* has tapered leaves and a notched leaf that is purple underneath. The flower has a sweet odor and is mostly identified by this.

Medicinal Uses and Preparation

Spatterdock and the fragrant white water lily have roots that have been used medicinally. One of their main uses was to decrease the sex drive. They are astringent and have been used to poultice swellings and to treat wounds, bleeding, boils, bruises, and inflammation. As with other plants of this astringent nature, they are given for diarrhea, mouth sores, and sore throats. Boiled spatterdock leaves or roots have a reputation for getting rid of pain.

The fragrant white water lily has also been a treatment for coughs, including that of tuberculosis. It has been used to treat infected glands and is used as a douche for yeast infections.

Food

The seeds of spatterdock can be parched or popped like popcorn. The inner kernel may be eaten or ground into flour. The roots can be boiled, buttered, and eaten.

The yellow lotus has a large root much like a banana that can be prepared in the manner of a sweet potato. The unrolled leaves may be cooked and eaten as a vegetable, and the unripe seeds can be eaten as is, cooked, or made into flour.

The fragrant white water lily also has leaves that can be eaten before they unroll. The buds, seeds, and roots may also be eaten.

Other Uses

The fragrant white water lily, with its sweet smell, was thought of by some ancient cultures as a pure woman rising from the muck of the water. The flower has been used to soften skin and as a perfume.

Current Interest

There is no scientific evidence that any of the treatments based on water lilies is effective. However, research on plants is not comprehensive.

Caution

Care should be taken when identifying the fragrant white water lily. There is at least one lookalike that is poisonous: It has rounded petals, and the leaves are green underneath. There is also little odor.

Another caution lies not in the plant itself, but in the water in which it is growing. In many places, water lilies are growing in polluted water, and this should be considered before using them.

INSECT CHASER

Water lilies may be attractive to people, but they can chase bugs away. One recipe for a sure extermination of bugs and cockroaches is to mash the roots of water lilies and soak them in milk (Reader's Digest, *Magic and Medicine of Plants*). The liquid is then spread along cracks and known bug trails. A small paintbrush can aid in doing this.

A Native American Indian remedy is to burn dried water lily root and use the smoke to drive off crickets.

Willow

Salix

USED TO TREAT

Arthritis

Calluses

Corns

Cramps

Dandruff

Diarrhea

Fever

Food poisoning

Hay fever

Headache

Heartburn

Insomnia

Neuralgia

Poison oak

Rheumatism

Sore throat

Stomachache

Tumors

Wounds

USED AS/FOR

Anti-inflammatory

Astringent

Blood tonic

Expectorant

The word *Salix* is Celtic for "near water" and applied to willows probably because most willows are found in swamps, at the edges of streams, or beside lakes. Both Native American Indians and the early settlers were familiar with the graceful tree. It was used for fires, furniture, and to make divining rods to find water. The trunks furnished tipi poles for the Plains Indians and support poles for the houses of those living close to water—and all the people used the medicine of the tree.

Medicinal Uses and Preparation

Listening to the willow and watching its gentle movements encourages relaxation. Add this to its other uses, and you have a double medicinal benefit.

The branches of young, smooth willows are gathered and may be tied together to dry. A basic tea can be made from the broken twigs. Cool it and take no more than a mouthful at a time. When the desired result has been achieved, stop taking it. Use no more than an ounce daily (Michael Moore, *Medicinal Plants of the Mountain West*).

Because willow contains some of the same ingredients as aspirin, it has much the same effect. It has long been used to relieve the pain of headaches and arthritis.

GROWING

Willow grows easily near water or damp ground and starts readily from cuttings.

226

Its added anti-inflammatory properties make it well suited to rheumatism and neuralgia. The bark is also an astringent and is therefore good as a gargle for sore throats. It is taken for hay fever, colds, fevers, and as an expectorant. Heartburn, stomach problems, diarrhea, cramps, and food poisoning are treated with the tea. Willow tea has also been a treatment for bladder inflammation, sleeplessness, dandruff, and as a blood tonic. Strong tea is also used topically on poison oak and fresh wounds. Many apply it to corns and bunions, and it was once used on cancers and tumors.

Other Uses

Willow is used to make baskets and wicker furniture. Willow twigs make a very good artist's charcoal. Because of the nature of the wood, it has been used to make artificial limbs. It has also been burned into charcoal and used in making gunpowder.

Current Interest

Depressed bone marrow function caused by chemotherapy has been increased by the use of the bark of *Salix alba,* the white willow. It has also been used in treating leukemia (Lesley Bremness, *Herbs*).

Caution

Willow should not be taken by pregnant women. Some people are allergic to the pollen. If you cannot take aspirin, you should not use willow. In sensitive individuals there may be a reaction. This could be in the form of a nosebleed, irritated stomach, and possibly other symptoms.

WILLOW WASH

1 cup willow bark
2 cups water

Place the bark and water in a pan, bring it to a boil, and simmer, covered, for 30 minutes. Let the mixture cool. This is for use on the skin in the case of ulcers, poison oak, bleeding, wounds, infected injuries, corns, and calluses. Use it as wash or a poultice.

Yarrow *Achillea Millefolium*

USED TO TREAT

Bladder infection

Burns

Diarrhea

Fever

Flu

Gas

Hemorrhoids

High blood pressure

Scrapes

Wounds

USED AS/FOR

Beer brewing

Disinfectant

Food

Menstrual regulation

Sedative

Beautiful in a bouquet or effective as a medicine, yarrow is a plant worth having. *Achillea* is found in most parts of the world. Native American Indians and settlers alike used it in medicinal treatments and for cosmetic purposes.

Medicinal Uses and Preparation

The strongest parts of the plant are the top branches, leaves, and flowers. These may be cut, washed, and dried either on paper or in a large paper bag. A basic tea is made from the fresh or dried plant. One to three cups daily is the usual dose.

Yarrow is frequently used as a stomach tonic, and the tea is drunk lukewarm. Diarrhea and the flu are treated with it. Yarrow aids in controlling menstrual bleeding and is given as a hot tea to break fevers. Some use it for lowering blood pressure, as a sedative, and to treat bladder infections. It is said to help ulcers, liver problems, gallbladder problems, gas, spasms, and to shrink hemorrhoids. It increases bile and decreases internal bleeding.

Yarrow helps with relaxation and difficulty in sleeping. It works especially well for women in menopause.

GROWING

This ferny-leaved plant makes an attractive border whether it is blooming or not; however, it is very invasive with its creeping rhizome. It should be moved every two or three years to keep it in control. The plants can be bought in most herb nurseries. I've seen many warnings that the plant will poison itself after being in one place for several years, but I have not found this to be the case. Mine just keeps growing and growing.

Achillea is a good first-aid plant. It should be washed and crushed for a poultice to put on a fresh cut, scrapes, or old wounds. Yarrow stops bleeding and helps prevent soreness in wounds. It is good to use when camping or hiking and is usually easily found. The Ute word for yarrow means "wound medicine." Another tribe looks to this plant for the treating of burns.

Food

The leaves can be chopped and added to salad. Yarrow has also been used in place of hops to brew beer.

Current Interest

Yarrow has been found to be anti-inflammatory and astringent. Yarrow tea has a calming effect and possibly works as an antibiotic.

Caution

Don't take more than is recommended or take yarrow over a long period of time because it tends to make the skin more sensitive to the sun. It should not be taken during pregnancy. Be moderate in using yarrow.

A LATIN NAME FROM THE GREEK

The Greek hero Achilles was supposed to have used yarrow to treat the wounds of his soldiers during the Trojan War.

Yucca

Yucca

A western movie would not seem authentic unless it had yucca showing up now and then. Just a picture of yucca flavors the mind with the Southwest; however, the plants are not confined there. The yucca population reaches into many other states. Long, sharp daggerlike leaves form a base for the long stem, which holds the tuliplike flower. Through the years yuccas have provided many a person with food, clothing, and medicine.

Medicinal Uses and Preparation

The medicine of the yucca plant is found in the root, which is usually dried for use. After digging the root, wash it well, dry it off, and split it lengthwise before drying.

Some Native American Indian tribes burned the root and used the smoke as a treatment. The dried root can be pounded, a bit of water added, and lather is formed when it is rubbed. This is used as a treatment for baldness and dandruff. A treatment for skin can be obtained by pounding the dry root with a rock and boiling it in a small amount of water. Grease is then added, and the mixture is heated and then cooled. This is reputed to work on skin problems, sprains, and sores. A decoction is used as an arthritis treatment.

USED TO TREAT

Arthritis

Dandruff

Skin problems

Sores

Sprains

USED AS/FOR

Basket weaving

Food

Hair growth

GROWING

Yucca is sold in most nurseries in the regions in which it can grow. It is frequently used in rock or cactus gardens.

Food

Yucca flowers, just before the bud opens, may be dipped in batter and fried. The seeds may be eaten, and in some species the fruit has the look and taste of a giant date.

Other Uses

Some yucca types have been crushed and put into small bodies of water. This stuns fish, which can then be picked up. The fibers from the leaves may be used to make fiber or rope, and the leaves can be made into baskets.

The pounded root is used to wash hair and skin. It is also used by some Native American Indian tribes to clean their woven goods.

The plant supplies commercial drug companies with substances to make certain medicines.

Current Interest

In the laboratory, a water extract of yucca root has proven effective against cancer in mice.

Tests have also shown a possible effectiveness against arthritis (Steven Foster and James A. Duke, *Eastern/Central Medicinal Plants*).

Caution

Yucca tea or decoction taken by mouth should be limited to a short period of time. It has the ability to irritate the bowels and can cause diarrhea in some people. It may also prevent some vitamins from being absorbed.

THE MOTH AND THE FLOWER NEED EACH OTHER

The yucca moth lives in yucca flowers and as an adult never eats. After her eggs are fertilized she gathers pollen and makes a ball, which she places in a spot behind her head. Then she carries it to another flower and lays her eggs in the seedpod. She climbs to the top of the pistil and pushes the ball into its top. When the babies hatch they go into a seed, where they eat and grow. There are plenty of seeds left for the reproduction of the yucca plant (Reader's Digest, *Magic and Medicine of Plants*).

231

Bibliography

Books

Ajilvsgi, Geyata. *Wildflowers of Texas*. Bryan, Tex.: Shearer
   Publishing, 1984.
Bremness, Lesley. *Herbs*. New York: Dorling Kindersley, 1994.
Coon, Nelson. *An American Herbal Using Plants for Healing*.
   Emmaus, Pa.: Rodale Press, 1979.
Densmore, Frances. *How Indians Use Wild Plants for Food,
   Medicine & Crafts*. New York: Dover Publications,
   1928.
Dobells, Inge N., ed. *Magic and Medicine of Plants*. New York:
   Reader's Digest, 1986.
Duke, James A. *Handbook of Northeastern Indian Medicinal
   Plants*. Lincoln, Mass.: Quarterman Publications, 1986.
———. *Handbook of Edible Weeds*. Ann Arbor, Mich.: CRC
   Press, 1992.
———. *The Green Pharmacy*. Emmaus, Pa.: Rodale Press, 1997.
Enquist, Marshall. *Wildflowers of the Texas Hill Country*.
   Austin, Tex.: Texas Lone Star Botanical, 1987.
Foster, Steven, and James A. Duke. *Eastern/Central Medicinal
   Plants*. Peterson Field Guides. Boston: Houghton
   Mifflin, 1990.
Galloway, Mary Regina Ulmer (as told by Mary U. Chiltoskey).
   Aunt Mary, Tell Me a Story. Cherokee, N.C.: Cherokee
   Communications, 1992.
Gibbons, Euell. *Stalking the Healthful Herbs*. Putney, Vt.: Alan
   C. Hood & Company, 1966.
Green, James. *The Herbal Medicine-Makers Handbook*.
   Forestville, Calif.: Wildlife and Green Publications,
   1990.

Hamel, Paul B., and Mary U. Chiltoskey. *Cherokee Plants—
Their Uses: A 400-Year-Old History*. Cherokee, N.C.:
Cherokee Communications, 1975.

Hylton, William H. *The Rodale Herb Book*. Emmaus, Pa.:
Rodale Press, 1974.

Keville, Kathi. *Herbs: An Illustrated Encyclopedia*. New York:
Friedman/Fairfax, 1994.

Kirkpatrick, Zoe Merriman. *Wildflowers of the Western Plains*.
Austin: University of Texas Press, 1992.

Kowalchik, Claire, and William H. Hylton (eds.) *Rodale's
Illustrated Encyclopedia of Herbs*. Emmaus, Pa.: Rodale
Press, 1987.

Lust, John B. *The Herb Book*. New York: Bantam Books, 1987.

Mooney, James. *James Mooney's History, Myths and Sacred
Formulas of the Cherokees*. Asheville, N.C.: Historical
Images, 1992.

Moore, Michael. *Medicinal Plants of the Mountain West*. Santa
Fe: Museum of New Mexico Press, 1979.

———. *Medicinal Plants of the Desert and Canyon West*. Santa
Fe: Museum of New Mexico Press, 1989.

———. *Los Remedios*. Santa Fe: Red Crane Books, 1992.

Ody, Penelope. *The Complete Medicinal Herbal*. New York:
Dorling Kindersley, 1993.

Peterson, Lee Allen. *Edible Wild Plants*. Peterson Field Guides.
Boston: Houghton Mifflin, 1977.

Phklow, Mannfried. *Healing Plants*. New York: Barron's, 1992.

Rohde, Eleanor Sinclair. *The Old English Herbals*. New York:
Dover Publications, Inc., 1971.

Silverthorne, Elizabeth. *Legends and Lore of Texas Wildflowers*.
College Station: Texas A & M University Press, 1996.

Skinner, Charles M. *Myths and Legends of Flowers, Trees, Fruit,
and Plants*. J. B. Lippincott Company, 1911.

Torres, Eliseo. *Green Medicine: Traditional Mexican-American
Herbal Remedies*. Kingsville, Tex.: Nievies Press, 1983.

Tull, Delena. *A Practical Guide to Edible and Useful Plants*. Austin: Texas Monthly Press, 1978.

Weiner, Michael A., and Janet A. Weiner. *Herbs That Heal*. Mill Valley, Calif.: Quantum Books, 1994.

Wickler, Wolfgang. *Mimicry in Plants and Animals*. New York: McGraw-Hill, 1968.

Wood, George B., and Franklin Bache. *The Dispensatory of the United States*. Philadelphia: Grigg & Elliot, 1836.

Papers and Periodicals

Blumenthal, Mark. "Herbal Industry and FDA Issue Chaparral Warning." *Herbalgram* # 28, 1993, 38–39.

Duke, James A. "Weeds? Or Wonder Drugs? *Organic Gardening*, July-August, 1994, 38–40.

McCaleb, Rob. "Herbal Help for Prostate Problems." *Herbs for Health*, Spring/Summer 1996, 26–28.

Salmon, Enrique. "Cures of the Copper Canyon: Medicinal Plants of the Tarahumara with Potential Toxicity." *Herbalgram* # 34, 1995, 43–54.

Webb, Ginger. "Benefits of Grape Seed Extract." *Herbalgram* # 38, 1997, 20.

Plant Index

General Index

kidney problems, 25, 86, 109,
190, 199, 211, 222
kidney stones, 45, 75, 88, 104,
209

labor contractions, 37, 196
laryngitis, 103, 104
laxatives, 12, 13, 15, 16, 37,
48, 53, 57, 75, 81, 83, 86,
104, 141, 148, 172, 176,
195, 202, 204, 206, 219
leather tanning, 81
leprosy, 202
lethargy, 222
leukemia, 160, 164, 180, 203,
227
leukorrhea, 59
lice, 123
linen, 86
liver problems, 48, 81, 96, 202,
228
liver purification, 12, 75, 83
liver tonics, 79
local anesthetic, 12, 13
love potions, 217
lung problems, 60, 169, 219

malaria, 32, 108, 111, 132,
196, 211, 212
measles, 22, 55, 97
memory loss, 125
menopausal problems, 52, 110,
186, 228
menstrual problems/regulation,
18, 23, 28, 34, 42, 43, 51,

52, 81, 88, 104, 107, 125,
129, 133, 143, 159, 171,
176, 186, 188, 192, 204,
209, 214, 216, 228
metabolic disorders, 85
migraines, 85, 191
milk flow, stimulation of, 216
modern drugs, 6
morning sickness, 158
mouse repellents, 189
mouth sores/ulcers, 12, 13, 28,
56, 65, 75, 137, 192, 207, 224
mouthwash, 55, 178, 181, 186,
193, 194, 210
muscle relaxants, 108, 131

narcotics, 114
Native Americans, healing
plants and, 5, 12, 22, 24,
27–28, 30, 34, 38, 44–45,
47, 56, 57, 59, 63–64,
69–70, 72–73, 80, 88, 92,
96, 99, 109, 111, 113, 118,
129, 134, 143, 161, 163,
173, 182, 190, 197, 212, 226
nausea, 28, 111, 125, 143, 180
nerves, 25, 125, 143, 155, 183,
216, 222
neuralgia, 158, 186, 190, 199,
227
nosebleed, 92, 159, 196

oil infusions, 9
ointments, 54, 68, 80–81, 111,
114, 137, 148

65, 70, 72, 75, 83, 96, 97, 99,
109, 119, 169, 171, 219
uterine problems, 142

vaccinia virus, 187
venereal diseases, 81, 119
vermifuge (parasite remover), 39
viruses, 25, 66, 120, 143, 164
vitamins, 81, 90, 122, 153–54,
174, 183, 184, 212, 219, 222

warts, 70, 75, 142, 162, 169,
171, 172, 206, 214

weight loss, 85
wheezing, 51
whooping cough, 180
wine, 98–99
wounds, 18, 19, 25, 38, 55, 58,
65, 76, 80, 85, 90, 96, 109,
132, 137, 159, 162, 169, 174,
197, 209, 217, 222, 224, 227,
229
wrinkles, 17, 214

yeast infections, 77, 104, 176,
187, 215, 224